MW01235671

The
Simplicity
of a
Practical
JESUS

Kirk Ratliff

Praying that God will bless you with an amazing understanding what He can do in your life and how much He loves you!

God Bless

Kirk & Kim Ratliff

ISBN 979-8-57402-718-9 Paperback

Copyright © 2017 by Kirk Ratliff

2nd Edition 2021

Kirk Ratliff
Email: jcskustomcreations@gmail.com

Printed in the United States of America

Contents by Title

Daily Devotionals

Foreward

"The purpose of my instruction is that all believers would be filled with love that comes from a pure heart, a clear conscience, and genuine faith" (1 Timothy 1:5, NLT; emphasis added).

The urgent cry of our Lord Jesus Christ is that the church would abandon it all and run to Him. That we would be the followers He desires us to be, forsaking the pleasures and desires our world and culture throw at us. For that to happen, we have to get back to consistent daily devotions in our lives. Time set aside to study, dig deep, and meditate on His word. To truly live Psalm 119:11, I have hidden your word in my heart that I might not sin against you.

I believe what Kirk offers in his book of daily devotions is an easy, simple concept in deepening our relationship with Jesus Christ. Let this book take you deeper, challenge, correct, and stretch you. My prayer for you as you read each day and chapter is that your heart would be soft and obedient to the things of Christ. That you find yourself falling more and more in love with your Creator and for His people. That what He is instilling and putting in your heart begins to move in action to our world around us. That we would be the answered prayer that Jesus prayed, "So now I am giving you a new commandment: Love each other. Just as I have loved you, you should love each other. Your love for one another will prove to the world that you are my disciples" (John 13:34-35; emphasis added).

"Work hard so you can present yourself to God and receive his approval. Be a good worker, one who does not need to be ashamed and who correctly explains the word of truth" (2 Timothy 2:15, NLT).

—Jamey Bridges

Acknowledgements

I am truly grateful for all that Jesus made available to me.

Thank you for your love, mercy, grace, and compassion. I am grateful that when others saw no worth or future for my life that you had a plan and purpose.

I am eternally grateful to my loving wife and her commitment to stand with me while encouraging me in all that God is doing in me. Kim is not only the most beautiful woman I know, but the greatest treasure God has entrusted me with. I love you, Kimme Cakes.

Thank you, Mom and Dad, for being the parents you are. Through good times and bad, Jesus has broken through the darkness and given life and restoration to our family. Thank you for your love and support. I love you!

I am thankful for Quay and Etoile, my spiritual parents. Due to their willingness to represent the fullness of all that Jesus is, I have become the man that God has called me to be. Thank you both for your faithfulness to God's Word and the calling that God has placed in your lives.

Thank you, Pastor Tim, for depositing the Word of God into my life so many years ago and encouraging me to be all that God's Word says that I can be. You are a true treasure.

Thank you, Pastor Jamie Bridges, for your dedication and willingness to walk in and represent the Word of God. Kim and I are grateful that God has caused our paths to cross. Thank you for leading us in truth.

To all the people in my life whom I have not mentioned, you are not forgotten, and I am grateful for all that you have contributed to sculpting my life and helping to fulfill my purpose in Christ.

Introduction

Jesus was an amazing teacher. He was simple and practical. Most of the people He spoke with on a daily basis were farmers and fisherman; people who had little or no education. When Jesus traveled, the people who were in the towns ahead of Him all knew of the works and words that He both performed and spoke. Jesus made a statement once that the kingdom of God was like a child and that we should have childlike faith. In other words, we need to keep things simple!

The religious leaders of the day or the educated hated and despised Jesus. Jesus took the message that men distorted and misrepresented and made it available for anyone who would listen. The only people who didn't believe in Jesus and constantly asked for a sign were the educated religious ones. They made the message about what we do rather than about what Jesus was asking us to believe. Jesus was never in need of or in search of people to listen to His message. In fact, many times, He would have to hide himself from the people in order to rest and regroup.

Here are some very basic principles that we can apply in our everyday lives that will not only draw people to Jesus for the great good of the gospel, but they will help us to be successful in our everyday journey as well.

We were created for three reasons. The first and foremost is to fellowship with the Father. If we look at Jesus's life many times, he went off to a quiet place to pray and spend time with the Father because He knew that without the Father, He could do nothing. In the same way as we spend time with God daily, the Bible states that we can do all things because Christ is our strength. When we try and accomplish our destiny and purpose in our own strength, we set ourselves up for failure, because in and of ourselves, we can do nothing.

The second part of our journey is our destiny or our salvation in Christ. When Adam and Eve were in the garden, they literally wanted for nothing. God provided for all their needs and gave them the best of everything. God would walk with them in the cool of the day and fellowship with them. Destiny in what Christ accomplished on the cross restores us to the fullness of God's provision in our lives and as we walk with and fellowship with Him, we are also empowered to fulfill our purpose in this earth. Our purpose is our vision or the job that God has for us on this earth.

The foundation of everyone's purpose is the same. Go into all the world and disciple others, loving them, and allowing them to experience Jesus in us and through us. The Bible states that it's not God's desire that any man perish but that all should have eternal life while being restored in Christ. The thing that is different about everyone's purpose is that we have all been given different gifts and abilities. When we take the Word of God and allow it to change our lives, empowering us to practice patience, goodness, mercy, compassion, faithfulness, and so forth in our everyday lives, we are literally allowing others to experience the fullness of God in us. When we add our gifts and abilities, it becomes the platform for who we can reach and what we can accomplish in Jesus. For example, for sixteen years I did collision, I was a body man and a painter. I embraced my abilities; I learned and applied as much as I could while doing my job with excellence. When I had customers who were rude and greedy, displaying attitude that was anything but appealing, I chose to walk in love and allow God to reach the lost and dying through me.

The next ten years, God gave me the opportunity to open a shop building hot rods and Harleys doing custom work. Again, I used every opportunity along with my abilities to advance the Gospel and love people. Every time I experienced success, I was able to reach more people. Our success isn't so we can say look what I did or who I am but rather it is a tool or an opportunity to reach the lost and dying while bringing hope to the hopeless.

The only thing that we can take to heaven with us is another soul. I can remember sitting in church during the praise and worship service and asking God to use me to not only reach the lost and dying but also to use me to finance the gospel around the world. I had recently been let go from my job and the enemy laughed stating, "How can you finance world missions, you can't even provide your own needs?" The truth is, God provides my needs, and I can do all things through Jesus because He is my strength. As I sat worshipping God, He gave me the idea to write this book and that I would be able to take the proceeds of this book and literally finance the gospel around the world. The task looked huge and impossible, but like many times in my life, I just put my faith and trust in Him. Every dime generated from this book will go to funding the gospel around the world.

This purpose of this book is twofold; it encourages others to know and understand their purpose and how to achieve it with excellence, and it also reaches the lost and dying with the gospel of Jesus Christ. Thank you, Jesus!

Jesus said that it wasn't His desire that any man perish but that all have eternal life through Him. The Bible states that there are two reasons that we fail as Christians. The first reason we fail is a lack of knowledge! Knowledge is power; it instructs us on who we are in Christ, it teaches us our rights, and it exposes the enemy and all his plans and schemes. Without the Word of God in our lives on a daily basis, we are destined for heaven but powerless and defeated on this earth to accomplish our purpose. This brings me to the second reason that God's people fail and that is a lack of vision or a lack of purpose. I can't have purpose until I have knowledge. Every reputable business has a vision or mission statement. This is what they want to accomplish with the gifts and abilities they possess. The cool thing about vision with God is the sky is the limit! The Bible states that in Him, we can do anything and that we are not limited by our abilities; in fact, He makes a way where there is no way.

So what is the deciding factor of what God will and can do through us? Obedience! The Bible states that if I am faithful in the small things, God will put me over bigger things. Many times in our lives, we want the bigger better deal but are not humble enough to walk in excellence in the small things in life, such as having a good attitude when someone speaks wrongly to us, doing our job with excellence when everyone around us isn't. Disciplining others isn't always what we can tell them it's what they see being displayed in our lives. We can't lead in truth if we first don't know the truth ourselves.

For many years, we as Christians have made salvation and Christianity something it was never designed to be. We have led people to believe that when they ask Jesus into their hearts that life will be candy and spice and all things nice. The Word of God never states we wouldn't have trials and tribulations; however, it does state that if we will draw close and rely on God, He will turn the bad situations around for His glory and our benefit. The Bible states that all things good or bad work together for our good because we love God and are called according to His purpose. Most people want to run when life gets hard, but true maturity in Christ empowers us to hold firm in the times of trouble because we know that God will not only bring us through, but He will strengthen and mature us in the process, giving us promotion to the next level.

For years, we as the church have made Christianity about how we dress and keep our hair; it has been about manmade rules and ideas that we thought would bring us closer to God, but in the end, it turned people away from the truth and isolated us as Christians. People were drawn to Jesus because Jesus never saw people's problems or shortcomings, but He always saw their potential in Him. The Bible states that love conquers all and that the love of God through us draws people to know and understand all that God has for them. Love finds no fault. Don't hear what I'm not saying; I'm not saying you will be popular with everyone, but people will be drawn to Jesus because we allow Jesus to live in us and through us.

I was raised in a church setting, attending Sunday morning, evenings, and Wednesday nights for the majority of my childhood. I attended Christian schools but was never sure how to fulfill my purpose in this earth. I learned a lot of great things and the foundations of what we as Christians are supposed to believe, but it wasn't until 1988 when I was arrested for robbing a gas station that an amazing man and woman of God began to mentor me in truth and the simplicities of God's love. I was facing a seven-year prison sentence, and my future was anything but bright. I was nineteen years old when I called on Jesus to come into my heart. I wasn't sure if God could even help my situation. As my mentors began to teach me the truth of God's Word while instructing me on how to apply it to my life, I then experienced the life-changing power of God's plan for my life. I was hooked! I read my Bible from cover to cover in the first three months. I read it through a second time in the next six months.

As I sought this amazing truth, God began to give me insight and understanding and a desire for His plan and purpose for my life. Second, I wanted everyone I meet come to know and understand the saving grace of Jesus Christ. I wanted their lives to be transformed as I was now experiencing. God gave me a peace that was so calming that as I surrendered to Him, I promised that if He would deliver me from my mess, I would serve Him; but if I went to prison, I would take His truth to anyone who would listen. I continued to read, pray, and search God out in my life with a hunger for whatever God would do in me, through me, and for me.

The time came for me to go before the judge, and as I stood there confident regardless of the outcome, I knew God was in control! The judge asked me to come to the side of his bench and he held in his hand a New Testament Bible. He said regardless if you take this or leave this, God has an amazing plan and purpose for your life, and with tears streaming down my face, I shared my God experience with him. I walked away that day with probation and as long as I finished my probation with no problems, the charges would be expunged from my record. Thank you, Jesus!

My mentors answered questions day after day, month after month, and sometimes three and four times a night as I would read and want to know God's truths for myself. I was saved but rough around the edges with lots of imperfections. This couple never pointed out my faults, they never saw me for my problems, but they always saw my potential in Christ. Quay and Etoile has always loved me right where I'm at — never judging and always encouraging. Love conquers all! This couple uses every opportunity to represent God's love while advancing the gospel daily. It was this practical display of who Jesus is and the simplicity of God's love that inspired me to be a mentor for the people God had placed in my life. The Bible states that God is love and that this same love conquers all!

In the book of Romans, it states that the goodness or the love of God through us will draw all men to a place of understanding of all that God is and all that He wants to do in them, through them, and for them. Simple! Living a successful Christian life is 95 percent of people seeing Jesus in us and 5 percent what we tell them. The greatest scheme of the enemy is offense at what others do or don't do, say or don't say. The good news is, God literally empowers us to overcome any tactics Satan may use to try and stop the flow of the most powerful truth the world will ever know, and that is God's love in us and through us.

The Bible states we should be quick to listen, slow to speak, and always try every situation according to the Word of God. When we do this, God not only prospers all our efforts, but he also takes the plans and schemes of what Satan meant for our destruction and turns them around, bringing glory and honor to His name while working it out for our benefit.

This book is a compilation of inspirations that God has given me over the years to encourage people in truth while giving them a practical application that allows them to experience the love of God through me. I am literally drawing many to the saving grace of Jesus Christ. Thank you, Quay and Etoile, for being my spiritual parents and allowing God's love, mercy, grace, and compassion to change my life forever. Thank you, Jesus, for being faithful, true, and just and entrusting me with the greatest asset—people's souls. All glory honor and praise to you, my Creator.

According to *Webster's* dictionary, this is the definition for inspiration; a divine influence or action on a person believed to qualify him or her to receive and communicate sacred revelation. The Bible states the power of life and death is in the tongue. Let your words be a healing balm in the lives of others.

Daily

Devotionals

Kirk Ratliff

Faith

Faith is the substance of things hoped for and the evidence of things not yet seen! (Hebrews 11:1). Okay, so how do we get faith? According to the Bible, faith comes from reading and applying the Bible to your lives! (Romans 10:17). Every day in our lives, we have a certain level of faith in many different things! For example, if I sit in a chair, I believe it will hold me; if I use the remote to turn the TV on, I believe that when I push the button, the TV will come on! We have thousands of things that we do every day that require us to believe before we can see the result! Again, I believe before I push the button on the remote that when I do, the TV will come on; however, I can't see the result if I don't act on what I believe!

Why is it that we can believe in so many things daily, but we can't believe that what God says in His Word, He will do! (Numbers 23:19). When we begin to read the Bible, it educates us on what God says is available in our lives. When I begin to speak those things daily as a confession, my mind will begin to learn, and the more I speak it, the clearer it becomes in my heart. As a result, we will begin to see the results of what we have been studying! For example, the Bible states that we are the head and not the tail, we are above and not beneath, that we are the apple of God's eye, and that we are righteous because of all that Jesus accomplished on the cross! (Deuteronomy 28:13).

If we are constantly speaking things that are contrary to God's Word, we will never see His promises manifested in our lives. Things like, I'm no good, no one loves me, I can't, I won't, I just don't know, so forth and so on. This type of behavior will only produce more feelings and situations that will produce more negativity in our lives! This is why God states that we should renew our minds daily by reading and applying His Word to our lives! (Romans 12:2, Ephesians 4:22-23). The issue of the Word not working comes when we read it once, and never speak it, or apply it!

Be diligent, if you truly want change and good things in your life, read your Bible daily, ask God to reveal all that He has for you and to open your eyes to the truth so that you can apply it to your life! God is faithful to do His part if you will do your part! (1 Corinthians 1:9). So seek Him in your life, spend time investing in your life through reading and applying His Word, and know that when it's all God, it will be all good!

Kim and I love you and are excited for you to experience all that God has in store for your life!

Facing the Giant

We all know the story of David and Goliath (1 Samuel 17). Goliath was an enemy of Israel and was nine feet tall. Fear had gripped Israel because they were focused on the size of the enemy. How many times do we have a problem arise in our lives and we accredit the severity of our problem to the attributes it presents? No matter what the size, shape, or name of the problem is, the problem isn't the issue. It is how we think and react to the problem that determines the outcome of the answer! (Proverbs 4:23).

The reason I am so adamant on reading our Bibles is because it trains us to think like God. When our thoughts line up with God, we are able to see God's potential rather than our abilities. In our own strength, we can do nothing, but through God, all things are possible because Christ is our strength! (Philippians 4:13).

David came along and was just a young boy but because he knew God and was in relationship with God. He knew all things were possible. The king wanted David to wear all different armors, but David already had all he needed (Ephesians 6:11). The confidence of who he was in God! As David approached Goliath, he asked, "Who are you that you come against the people of the God Most High? Today, I will slay you in the name of 'The Lord.'" David took his slingshot and knocked Goliath out, and then took the sword that Goliath had threatened the people of God with and cut his head off. Don't misunderstand, the victory wasn't won by a sling shot, or a sword, it was won because David understood who he was in God. The good news is, God is the same now as he was then, and he isn't a respecter of persons (Hebrews 13:8). What God did for David, He will do for us (Romans 2:11). We first need to understand that the victory is God's. When we stand on the Word of God, the power to overcome will be made available to us. Any other way just won't work!

We need to read our Bibles, train our brain, and seek God in our lives (Matthew 6:33, Luke 12:31). "We need to quit talking about the problem and start speaking the Word of God over the problem (Psalms 119:105). This is the only way to ensure victory. When God works through us, He does what others say can't be done! (Philippians 2:13).

Kim and I love you, have a great day!

Fear Not

FEAR is False Evidence Appearing Real. The BIBLE or Basic Instructions Before Leaving Earth states 365 times fear not! I thought it significant that God would tell us this 365 times. That's one time for every day of the year. We should not spend one minute of one day fearful of what might be or what could be!

The Bible states that perfect love cast out fear (1 John 4, 1 John 4:18). God is this perfect love and lives in us. Fear is never based on truth but rather on facts. An example of this might be that our economy is unstable and this is a fact. God's Truth always overcomes or trumps a fact.

The truth is, God supplies all of my needs according to His riches in Christ Jesus! (Philippians 4:19). The world is full of facts, and most people are under the power of those facts because they know no truth. Why are so many Christians who have access to truth not walking in truth? Because it's easier to walk by what we see.

Facts always paint a picture. Facts are always willing to accommodate our every fear. Truth requires trusting in what you can't see. God's Word is true, faithful, and just. God obviously knew that every day, we would be faced with facts based on fear. That's why God encourages us 365 times and says fear not! Don't lie down and settle for less when God says you can have it all. We can do all things through Christ because He is our strength!

Kim and I love you. Have a great day.

Fear or Faith

Fear always demands a need to control people. Faith gives us the freedom to trust God. The Bible states that God is not a man that He should lie and that we can put our faith and trust in every word that comes from His mouth! (Numbers 23:19). When we are disciplining others, it's easy to get caught up in fear of what could happen when we see the plans and schemes of the enemy trying to work in their lives. The deception is that if we allow worry and fear of what could happen, it only snares us into thinking that by trying to control the situation, we can keep our student from stumbling (Job 3:25).

The great part about trusting God and all of His wisdom is knowing that the work He started in us, He will finish! (Philippians 1:6). It totally removes all the stress of trying to control the outcome of someone else's salvation. I have led many to come to know and understand the saving grace of Jesus Christ. They are always full of ideas and notions of what and who God is and what they can and can't do. All based on a lack of knowledge of God's Word. People are led by example.

So lead by example! Never stop praying for them. Allow your student to experience the power of God speaking to them in a beautiful growing relationship. Our job is to lead people to Jesus and allow our example to educate them in what is pleasing to God. He is the Shepherd and He will watch over, guide, and protect them. So let go and let God because when it's all God, it's all good!

Have a great day and know Kim and I love you and are excited for what God is doing in you, threw you, and for you!

Follow the Instructions

I recently heard someone blame God for their misfortune! I realize that this is just a lack of understanding on their part. Satan is the author of confusion (1 Corinthians 14:33), and he comes to steal, kill, and destroy (John 10:10). Jesus came to give an abundance of life. We can't see God's goodness if we see God as the source of our pain!

Oftentimes, we as people want to serve God only when it suits us, but we want the full benefit of a full-throttle relationship! If we put flower and vanilla and sugar and all the ingredients needed to produce a cake in the oven, the heat will transform my mix of ingredi- ents into something desirable and pleasing! Some might say, "Well, I just don't think I need all of these ingredients," "I don't have time to bake for thirty minutes, I'll just do ten minutes," "Who needs an oven glove, I'll just grab it with my hand," "We know that nothing good will come from any of this. It's a mess waiting to happen." We can't blame anyone, because we didn't do what was required to get the full potential of the situation!

God is no different! God has an amazing plan and purpose for our lives He has good things for us. God desires for us to know the full potential of all that is promised in His Word. Here is the catch. God requires us to walk out His Word, seeking Him daily, trusting Him full, and surrendering our lives, wants, and desires to His plan and purpose! (Philippians 2:12). There will be fiery darts that are shot at us in life. When we stand behind the shield that is provided, we can trust that our safety is in God's hands. Don't step out from behind God's shield and then blame God when the arrows hit you! We need to read our Bibles and be quick to do whatever the Bible prompts us to do. Seek God daily and know that He only wants the best for us!

Kim and I love you and are cheering for you. Have a great day!

Food for Thought

America is the most fed but most undernourished country in the world today. We have fast food on every corner with meals that have no nutritional value but are not short on calories. Fast food is unhealthy, leaving us sick and craving for more. As I was sitting here thinking about this, I realized that our spiritual lives are often like a fast-food experience. We only take enough to leave us malnourished and wanting more. Sometimes, we never really take the time to dig in deep finding the truths that give us the nutrition we really need to accomplish greatness in our lives and the lives of others. We don't allow God to transform our lives filling us with peace, joy, and His life-changing love. We are surrounded by end- less opportunities to help others find and experience their purpose in this life, but we don't have purpose in our own lives.

I often ask the question, are you reading your Bible? The answer I usually get is, "I don't have time." We make time for all sorts of things in our lives but yet for the very thing that will change our lives while empowering us for greatness we don't. We often fill our lives with things that have a Christian appearance but no substance. We ask God why our lives are such a mess and when will He fix our problems. Before Jesus died, he said it is finished (John 19:30). God has done all that He is going to do! God is waiting for us to educate ourselves feeding our spirit with His Word, while walking in the fullness of all that He has provided through the death, burial, and resurrection of His son.

Don't have a fast-food relationship with God. We have a church on every corner, we have every tool available for greatness, but we live our lives powerless. If we don't have a plan for our future, then our future will be a repeat of our past. We need to take the time to read our Bibles, put Jesus first in our lives, and the rest is just history.

Kim and I love you and want great things for you. Have a great day.

Free Doesn't Mean No Effort Required

I am amazed at the mind-set we often have when serving God. When I have a job, I'm required to not only come to work but also to do my job when I am there. If I didn't do my job or didn't come to work, I would be out of line to play the victim if I got fired. If I were a student and didn't go to class or even do my homework, it would be foolish for me to feel slighted if I failed.

Serving God is no different. Actually, our entire life should be a result of God's faithfulness because of our diligence to do our part. I am also amazed at the lack of balance and how we get so off centered when it comes to serving God. Some say it's all about grace. Others say it's all about works. The truth of the matter is, works in faith is the perfect balance of God's desire for our lives (James 2:14-26). True faith is a result of reading and applying the Word of God to our lives.

As we become whole in our thinking, renewing our minds daily through the washing of the Word, we are equipped with the nutrients that allow faith to grow in our hearts. The Word states that the issues of life flow from the heart and the way we think directly affects the outcome of the issues in our lives (Proverbs 4:23). True faith has the ability to accomplish anything due to the fact that faith is a result of God's love and a product of His faithfulness. The Bible instructs us in many areas that we have responsibilities if we are going to experience the fullness of His faithfulness. For instance, the Word instructs us to study to show ourselves approved (2 Timothy 2:15). Approved of what? Not that we have God's approval so to speak, but rather when the trials of life come, we are equipped with the answers to overcome the opposition and be successful in life. The Bible instructs us to put on the full armor of God (Ephesians 6:10-18). The armor is made up of God's full provision not only to see us through the battle but allowing us to come through unharmed. This is why the Word states even when we go through the fire, we will not be burned and when we go through the deep waters, we will not drown (Isaiah 43:2).

The Word instructs to have a giving heart (Luke 6:38, 1 John 3:17, James 2:15). When we give and we are grounded in love, we are a perfect reflection of Jesus. Why? Because he first loved and out of that love, He gave all of Himself so that we can experience all that He is and has for us. When God states give and it will be given to us pressed down shaken together and running over, most people use this as a money scripture. However, when we are overflowing with all of God's goodness, we literally provide the answers to all who have no hope. The truth, which is Jesus, lives in us and empowers us to lead others to the fullness of God's faithfulness.

The Bible instructs us to draw close to God, resist the devil and he will flee (James 4:7). When do we draw close? Most of us wait until we are surrounded by Satan's opposition before we seek God. We should seek God daily so that in those times of opposition, we are strong enough to resist Satan's plans and schemes for our lives. The Word has instruction for every area of our lives and when we apply His wisdom to our lives, we are empowered to walk in the fullness of all that God wants to do in us, through us, and for us (2 Timothy 3:16). So here is the skinny! If we don't seek God and we don't read and apply our Bible to our lives, then we are literally bound and limited to Satan's ploys for our lives. The only outcome in our lives is defeat. It's not God's fault, it's not because the Word doesn't work; it's strictly because we didn't do our part. God's Word is faithful, true, and just, and His promises are "yes" and "amen" (2 Corinthians 1:20). The good news is this, that when we are faithful to do our part, God is faithful to do His part. In fact, Jesus stated on the cross, *it is finished*! (John 19:30). There is nothing else to do; it's already been done. The only thing left to do is to do our part.

Kim and I love you and are excited for you to experience the faithfulness of God's provision for your lives, empowering you for greatness. Have a great day.

God Is the Same Yesterday, Today and Forever

Knowing that God never changes, let's look at Jesus's return and see if there is a pattern in the Bible validating His return! In Genesis 7, the Bible talks about a wicked and perverse people. He called Noah to build an ark. God was going to pour out His wrath on this earth. God not only wanted to save the animals but His righteous followers as well.

Fast forward a bit and look at Sodom and Gomorrah (Genesis 19). God was fed up with the wickedness of the people and was going to pour out His wrath. Prior to judgment, God removed His faithful, Lot and his family. Any time that we see God pouring out His wrath in the Word of God,

He always removes His faithful first! When we go forward again to the New Testament, God states that as it was in the days of Noah, so shall it be in the coming of Jesus (Matthew 24:37, Luke 17:26-30). Like the story of Noah, God will not only pour out his wrath but just as before, God will make sure that His people are safe! Hence the rapture! One day in the future, Jesus will return and gather up His righteous. Then He will pour out His wrath on this earth. If you do not know Jesus as your Savior, I encourage you to ask Him into your heart today! God has an awesome plan and purpose for your life (Jeremiah 29:11). Choose to seek God first and the rest is all good!

Kim and I love you. Have a great day.

God Makes a Way

I have been very blessed to speak into many lives through this daily devotional. I have many who subscribed, and I would like to share one of their stories so that you can hear how God's Word is working in their lives.

Hi, my name is Denny. I have been receiving this daily devotional for a while now. Eight months ago, I was strung out on meth, and my life was hopeless. I started coming to church where my wife and I met Kirk and Kim. Kirk was always telling us of the power of God's Word and His faithfulness to perform His Word in our lives. We started getting these devotionals and reading our Bible as a couple and seeking God in our lives. When I was using meth, I had some charges that were still pending, and I knew that I would have to face my charges. Kirk and Kim would always remind us that God is in control and that He makes a way when there seems to be no way. Last Friday, I was arrested and was being held on a seventeen-thousand-dollar cash only bond. Prior to this, Kirk said use every opportunity to advance the gospel. Kirk reminded me that if I had to be locked up, then someone there needed to hear about God's saving grace. Every night in jail, I held a Bible study as Kirk and Kim were encouraging my wife. My situation seemed impossible. Today, just four days later, I was released with no bond and was in time to attend church. God made a way where there was no way! As I was leaving jail, I told the inmates that the Word of God is true. Read it, apply it, and live it! Thank you, Jesus, for all that you have done for my wife and I. We love you and give all the glory, honor, and praise to your holy name!

The Simplicity of a Practical Jesus

This is just one testimony! God is not a respecter of persons what He did for this couple He will do for you! (Romans 2:11). God's Word is faithful, true, and just. God's promises are "yes" and "amen".

Kim and I love you and are excited for you to experience and see God work in your lives as He did in with this couple! Have a great day.

God's Image

God made us in His image! (Genesis 1:27). So what does that mean? Let's take a minute and see what the Word of God has to say about it! The Word says that God is mighty (Joshua 4:24). God has no enemy that can overcome Him. God is creative, compassionate, loving, all powerful, never defined by circumstances (John 1:3, Colossians 1:16). God has the power to change any and all circumstances. God owns everything therefore He is wealthy (Psalms 50:10). God empow- ers others with truth (1 Corinthians 15:9-10), and He is our strength (Psalms 46). God never stops looking for opportunities to display His faithfulness. It sounds to me that God is the perfect representation of a can-do attitude!

Let's sweeten the deal! We are created in God's image the perfect reflection of His Word. He gave His son Jesus to pay the price so we can have right standing with Him (1 Peter 1:20, John 3:16). God also gave us the ability to overcome any and all obstacles that try and get in our way!

The Bible states that through God's love and Jesus's sacrifice, we can do *all* things. Nothing is impossible! So we have salvation with the promise of eternal bliss. What are you doing with all the ability that you have been created with? Christianity is all about doing the impossible. We are empowered to do the impossible all for the sole purpose of reaching the lost and dying and helping them to come to know and understand God's saving grace. We help others to understand their ability for greatness. One day, we will stand before God, and we will have to give an account of what we did with all we were given! Live your life on purpose.

Fulfill your purpose in Christ and change the world as we know it. God's ability and your willingness makes for the greatest success any one can ever experience!

Kim and I are super excited for you to experience all that God wants to do in you, threw you, and for you. Have a great day!

Good Instruction

The Bible states that we are the righteousness of God in Christ set apart and made whole by all that Jesus died to accomplish on the cross (2 Corinthians 5:21). So what does it mean to be made whole? The Bible instructs us on how to prosper in every area of our lives experiencing the fullness of God's goodness. God's Word teaches us how to be finan- cially stable, how to live healthy, while instructs us what we should and shouldn't eat. God teaches us how to be emotionally whole. The wholeness of God for our lives includes emotional, mental, physical, and spiritual well-being. I don't know one person who doesn't want this kind of life! God's Word is true, faithful, and just. His promises are "yes" and "amen" (2 Corinthians 1:20), and He watches over His Word to perform it. So as we begin to read and apply God's Word in thought, word, and deed, our lives will become a result of God's faithfulness. God watches over His Word to perform it (Jeremiah 1:12). His Word never returns void, it always accomplishes what it was sent to do (Isaiah 55:11). We need to read it, learn it, apply it, and speak it. The Bible states that when we pray according to God's Word, He not only hears our prayers but He also answers them! (1 John 5:14). So why is a life that is made whole so important? It not only gives us peace of mind, freedom to enjoy life, and the assurance of God's love, but it also empowers us to help others come to know and understand the awesomeness of God's faithfulness. This is Christianity in a nutshell—experience God's wholeness while empowering us in teaching others that they too can be made whole.

Kim and I are so very blessed to encourage each of you in your lives and are super excited to see you walk in the fullness of God's Word. We love you guys and couldn't be prouder of you!

Good Morning

I was sleeping in this morning when the phone rang. I thought it was my alarm clock, but in fact, it was someone from our church family. I picked up the phone concerned there might be a problem when I was greeted with "Good morning!" It was my good friend Dave and his beautiful bride Angie. I could hear the excitement in Dave's voice as he stated that he didn't want anything but rather they just wanted to say, "Have a great day and we love you guys!" Dave began to tell me about a book that he was reading on how to achieve God's purpose for our lives and how he had discovered some pretty cool things in his daily Bible studies. Kim and I have been mentoring this couple regularly and were very excited for them to experience all that God wanted to do in them, through them, and for them.

This is an example of the power of God's love and how lives are changed when we take the time to encourage others while mentoring them in the Word of God. When we sow into the lives of others, it brings such a rewarding feeling of satisfaction. The last thing Jesus said while ascending to heaven was go into all the world and make disciples of all people! (Mark 16:15).

The purpose of this story isn't to ring our own bell but to encourage others to make a difference in the lives around us. Take the time to mentor others in the Word of God. When we don't read our Bibles, we don't know who we are or what God has provided for us. We can't lead others in truth if we first don't know truth ourselves! The truth of God's Word empowers us to lead others and remain free from the plans and schemes that Satan has for our lives. Keep Jesus first and choose to walk in God's amazing love. Change the world as we know it. Love conquers all!

Love always, Kirk and Kim.

Good Night

Good night to all my family on social media. May the angels watch over you as you sleep. We are precious in God's eyes. God loves us more than we know, and His mercies are new every morning (Lamentations 3:22-23). If you are in error or have made mistakes today, don't beat yourself up or allow the devil to beat you up either. Rather just talk to God before you sleep and allow the mercies of God to fill your life. Know that God is excited to call us friend, and He has an amazing plan and purpose for our lives. Many blessings to you and yours.

Much love from Kirk and Kim

Eternity Is Forever

I got a call about twenty minutes ago that my friend of twenty-six years had passed away! I find myself looking back over the years and asking myself what kind of an example was I in his life (1 Corinthians 11:1, Titus 2:7). Did he see Jesus in me? (Matthew 5:14-16, Ephesians 5:1-2, Galatians 2:20) My friend was very opinionated when it came to God and salvation. I can't say I know for sure where he will spend eternity! It chills me to even think about it! Life is short and eternity is forever (Psalms 39:5-6, 90:12, 144:4; Ecclesisates 1:2-4, 6:12; James 4:14; Proverbs 27:1).

Do you know where you will spend eternity? (1 John 2:17, John 3:16). The only way to know that heaven is your home is to invite Jesus into your heart, putting Him first in your life (Romans 6:23, Psalms 139:23-24). If you don't know Jesus, I encourage you to ask Him into your heart today (Romans 6:23, 10:9,13; Acts 2:21,38; Revelation 3:20; 1 John 1:9). Just say, "Jesus, come into my heart and help me to know and understand your plan and purpose for my life, amen!" Don't procrastinate! We just never know when our time will be up. It is never too late, God is with us till our last breath (2 Samuel 14:14; Ephesians 5:15-17; Psalms 48:14,107).

Kim and I love you. Have a great day!

Greatness

A willing heart is all that is required for greatness! Another word for willing is faithful. We were created for destiny, purpose, and greatness. Through our relationship with Christ Jesus, we are more than conquerors (Romans 8:37). The Bible states that we can do *all* things through Christ because He is our strength! (Philippians 4:13). For me, the coolest part of being friends with the Creator of the universe is, there is no limitation to what God can and will do in my life. The thought that I was created and destined to enjoy a friendship with the Creator of all things is amazing. The benefits are even more amazing!

The only thing God requires of us is that we use what He gives us as tools to reach the lost and the dying while loving the brokenhearted. Wow! The only person that will ever keep us from achieving greatness in our lives is us! The two things that will keep us from God's best is an unwilling heart or not exercising our abilities to dream big!

The Bible states that God seeks throughout the earth for a faithful heart that He can pour out His blessings on (2 Chronicles 16:9). So today, God's mercies are new. The rest of our lives can be the best of our lives. God states that the latter will be greater than the former (Hag. 2:9). Let's start living our lives like the world changers that we were created to be. We need to allow the blessings of God to consume our lives!

Kim and I love you and expect great things for your lives. Have a great day!

Help

Have you ever met someone who was always in need but never did anything to help themselves? Every time you saw them coming, it's like you just want to pretend you didn't see them and walk the other direction! It's not that they are a bad person. It's just for once you wish they would take the steps to fixing their problem without constantly draining others with their emotional instability.

The Bible states that the truth will set us free (John 8:32). Truth empowers us to walk in freedom from debt, sickness, poverty, mental and emotional distress, and anything else that is contrary to the promises of God for our lives. When Jesus walked the earth, it was the love of the Father through Him that allowed greatness to manifest in Jesus's life. Jesus said that we will do even greater things than He did! (John 14:12). Wow! Does this happen just because? No!

Greatness is a provision that is given to us through all that Jesus accomplished on the cross. It's what we choose to do with that greatness that gives us the ability to walk in truth while empowering us to set others free! When we choose to be needy and unwilling to walk in God's truth, our lives are robbed of the potential we have in Christ Jesus. Let's be honest, nobody likes a Willy or Wendy Whiners! The Bible states that all men are drawn to God when we allow truth of God's love to flow freely in our lives, affecting the lives around us. We can be pitiful or powerful; the choice is 100 percent ours!

Kim and I love you and are super excited to see God's greatness fulfilled in you. Have a super awesome day!

Lukewarm, Red Hot, or Ice Cold - Which Are You?

The Bible is very specific about what our lives should and shouldn't be. The Bible states that if we are not for God, then we are against Him! (Luke 11:23). So what does it mean to be for God? Our lives should be a reflection of God's love, His grace, and His mercy. We should build our lives on the truth of God's Word. This allows us to shine our light in this dark world, setting the captives free from sin and death. The Bible states that the love of God through us draws all men to know and understand the saving grace of Jesus Christ (Romans 2:4). When we allow the Word of God to sculpt our lives in the way we think, how we speak, and how we act, we are literally empowered for greatness.

So let's look at what a cold life looks like! I spent about an hour on social media watching different interviews with celebrities of all aspects. Movie stars, musicians, and entertainers who all claimed to have sold their souls to Satan for fame and fortune. Why would Satan want to promote and bring success to anyone's life? Satan stated that he wanted to be like God and be worshipped! (Isaiah 14:14). The Bible states what good does it do to gain all this world has to offer but lose our own soul (Mark 8:36). Satan is determined to use celebrities of all walks of life to deter people from serving God. Why? Because he also knows that if you're not for God, you're against Him. Satan wants to steal as many souls as he can, imprisoning them for eternity and keeping them from experiencing God's love.

So what does it mean to be lukewarm? Jesus stated that if we are lukewarm, He will spit us out of His mouth (Revelation 3:16). The world would say that there is not only a grey area in serving God but many shades of grey! Lukewarm states I believe in God, but my life is my life. To do nothing is the same as being wrong! The Bible states that a wise man wins souls and desires to set the captives free (Proverbs 11:30). When we stand before God and are not saved, we will have to give account of our sins. When we are saved and Jesus is our Lord and Savior, we will have to give account of what we did or didn't do with His Word! Are you allowing God's Word to help you reach your full potential in Christ Jesus? We should allow our light to shine through our words, thoughts, and actions. Is the love of God flowing through you allowing the lost and the dying to see Jesus in you? God has an amazing plan and purpose for our lives (Jeremiah 29:11). The only way we will see God's plans fulfilled in our lives is by seeking God daily and allowing His Word to make us all that He wants us to be!

Kim and I love you. Have a great day and keep Jesus first.

How Are We Limiting God?

What has God asked you to do? When Jesus went to Mary and Martha's due to Lazarus's untimely death, they faulted Jesus stating if you had been here, Lazarus wouldn't have died (John 11:1-44). It amazes me how we limit God's abilities. The sisters knew Jesus could heal Lazarus, but they didn't think Jesus could raise Lazarus from the dead. What problems are we experiencing in our lives and are limiting God in what He can do?

As Jesus walked up to the tomb, He asked the people to roll away the stone! Here, Jesus is going to give life to a dead guy who already smells because it's been four days but asks the people to roll the stone away. Why not just add to the miracle and roll the stone as well? Because when God is working miracles out in our lives, He requires us to do our part. You might say, "What is my part?" As we read and apply the Word of God in our lives, His plan and direction become clear as to what God requires of us. Also, as Jesus raised Lazarus from the dead, He said, "Lazarus, come forth!" Even Jesus was specific in the task at hand. Why? Because Lazarus wasn't the only person in that tomb, and if Jesus would have said come forth, then the whole tomb would have been emptied!

God wants to raise parts of your life, but other areas He wants to remain dead. So learn to be specific when using the authority that has been given to you through all that Jesus accomplished on the cross. Never put God in a box. The Scripture states that through Christ, all things are possible (Philippians 4:13). Learn your place through God's Word; always be flexible and willing to do your part. God will do the rest!

Have a great day and always remember Kim and I love you and are cheering for you!

If I Could Turn Back Time

I was watching a movie about a guy who found a wormhole in time, and he went back and tried to stop some bad things from happening. The more he tried to fix the wrongs, the worse the problem became. The Bible states that we are but a vapor on this earth (James 4:14). Our time is very limited in the grand scheme of eternity. The Bible never promises us that we won't experience hard times and opposition. The Bible even states that tomorrow is guaranteed to no man. God states that before we were in our mother's womb, He knew us (Jeremiah 1:5).

God has a plan and purpose for each and every one of us. Our destiny can only be defined when Jesus is the foundation of who we are. The reason the Bible goes into great length of who we are and what Jesus accomplished for us on the cross is so that we can put our faith and trust in Him and successfully accomplish the fullness of His plan for our lives. This is why the Bible states that the birds of the air don't worry for what they will eat or where their provision is coming from and because of this, they are now free to be all that they were designed to be (Matthew 6:26-34). When our faith and trust are in God regardless of our situation, we are functioning completely in the full potential of the amazing plan that God has for our lives.

Way too often, we worry and concern ourselves with temporal things such as provision, status, accomplishments, success, and on and on. When we realize that all those things are in Him and that our footsteps are divinely ordered, then none of that really matters. In reality, worry hinders us from accomplishing all that we are to accomplish in the few short years that we are on this earth.

The Bible states seek God first and everything else will be added (Matthew 6:33). We are also encouraged not to worry but rather to cast our care on Him because He cares for us (1 Peter 5:7). The Bible states to plan our lives as if we have forever but live our lives as if today was the last. How many of us would be worried about provision if today were the last? We wouldn't, and that's the whole point. Our life and being when in Him is following His plan and purpose, and we can only function to the fullness and experience the vastness of His plan when our faith and trust are in Him. So let go and let God because when it's all God, it's all good. B-asic I-nstructions B-efore L-eaving E-arth—Bible—if you want to succeed and see all that God has for yourself, study His Word.

Kim and I love you and pray that you experience and reach your full potential in Christ. Have a great day.

I'm Not Where I Want to Be,
But I'm Not Where I Used to Be!

We need to be in constant motion when seeking God and cultivating our relationship with the Creator. Have you ever heard the expression, "Rome wasn't built in a day"? Our walk with God is a process and as long as we are moving forward, we can be sure we are not going backwards.

Compromise is a slippery slope that has one destination—destruction! Satan is hard at work. His desire is to keep us from reading and applying God's truths to our lives. If he can't keep us from truth, then He distorts the truth or misrepresent it. Whether no truth or misrepresented truths, both are powerless! Satan sees our potential in Christ and knows that if we get the big pictures and realize our worth and potential in Christ, then we are literally unstoppable. Satan uses compromise because it is gradual and most times undetectable. If you put a frog in a pot of water and gradually begin to heat the water, that frog will sit there and literally boil to death because it's gradual, and it doesn't sense danger. Don't allow compromise to steal your dreams, kill your potential in Christ, and destroy your relationship with our Creator.

When we take inventory daily making sure that God is the center of all that we are, then we will reach our full potential while experiencing the fullness of God's love, mercy, grace, and compassion. When our lives become the reflection of all that God is, then we are literally empowered to set others free, giving them the gift of eternal life. God's plan is greater than we can think or imagine (Ephesians 3:20-21). So as we start or end our day, know that God is waiting to hear from us. He is excited to call us friends and has great plans for us. God is the perfect friend He chooses to see our potential over our faults, and His main desire is to see us prosper in all that He is.

The Simplicity of a Practical Jesus

Kim and I love you and are just as excited for the plans that God has for your life. Have a great day

Is Your Glass Half Empty or Half Full?

I recently took a job and never thought in a million years it would just be for a couple months. My plan looked a lot different. The Bible states that God's ways are not our ways, and His thoughts are not our thoughts (Isaiah 55:8). We also need to keep in mind that our footsteps are divinely ordered (Psalms 37:23) and God's Word is a lamp unto our feet (Psalms 119:105). When we live our lives in Him, there is no such thing as a setback but rather all things work together for my good, making Satan's setback God's setup for promotion. In the short time I was at this job, I was able to share the Word of God with several people. I was able to lay hands on a young mother to be as she had a tumor in her uterus. I prayed for her healing and to add to that, I introduced her to her Creator and was able to mentor her in truth.

The greatest commodity in this earth is another soul. Satan wants me to think I have failed due to the circumstances of the short time at this job. My focus isn't on the things of this world, it's on eternity and all that Jesus accomplished on the cross. Everything in life can have a negative, but when we are grounded in Christ Jesus, that negative becomes a positive. The Bible states that no matter what Satan uses as harm if we will trust God and apply His Word, then God takes Satan's negative and makes it a positive. All things good or bad work together for our good because we love God and are called according to His purpose.

There is nothing greater than giving the gift of eternal life to someone who is lost and dying! The Bible states that all of heaven rejoices when someone finds salvation and enters into relationship with their Creator. When we are faithful in the small things, then God puts us in charge of great things. Quit looking at adversity as failure and begin to walk in the fullness of God's Word. See yourself as God sees you, an overcomer in Christ empowered to do the impossible. We are the apple of God's eye and when we plant ourselves in Him, there is no such thing as a negative. Paul stated that even death was a positive because to be absent from the body would put us in the presence of God (2 Corinthians 5:8).

Kim and I love you and are grateful for all that God is doing in you, through you, and for you. Keep the faith and fight the good fight and together, we can change the world. Have a great day.

John Knew!

In the book of John, we see John's understanding and his perspective of who Jesus was and the validity of Jesus's ministry. The reason John understood the reality of Jesus's identity was because, for one, John knew the Word of God. The Word of God defined who John was hundreds of years before John was even born, states that John would be a voice calling from the desert, and that he would be clothed in camel's hair and eat wild locust (Isaiah 40:3). The difference between John and the religious leaders of the day was John not only knew who he was according to the Word, but he also had an open heart. The religious leaders of the day knew the Word but were not willing to truly know God in their hearts. Later in John's life, he was imprisoned for giving his opinion regarding the king's sin and also judging the king's sin in his heart.

People know what sin is; we as Christians don't need to go around pointing out the obvious. The Bible states we should not judge others because when we do, we will find ourselves being judged (Matthew 7:1-6). When we judge others, we are operating out of pride. The Bible is clear that pride comes and then we fall (Proverbs 16:18). We think that because their sin is not ours that we are qualified to point the finger at them. The beautiful part of walking in God's love is, true love finds no fault (1 Corinthians 13). Why? It's not our job to judge, it's our job to love and through the fact that pure love conquers all, we are empowered to reach the lost and the dying, giving them hope of salvation and God's promises. When we begin to judge, we open the door for Satan to have a right of passage to bring wrong situations, as John was facing being imprisoned.

When John the Baptist was in prison, he sent two of his disciples to visit Jesus for the purpose of asking an important question. He asked Jesus, "Are you the Messiah or is there another?" See, when we operate outside of God's will for our lives and find ourselves in bad or wrong situations, it opens us up for doubt and unbelief. Ultimately, because John was outside the will of God due to His judgmental attitude, it cost him his life and shortened His ministry or God's plan and purpose for John's life. God had such an amazing purpose for John's life, and it was evident to those around him. The religious leaders of the day asked John if he was the Messiah or even Elijah. That is a profound statement. Elijah had been gone from the face of the earth for hundreds of years and for them, to think that John was the embodiment of this man of past is a pretty loud statement. On the other hand, for people to question John as to being the Messiah is even more profound.

People might not understand God's plan for your life, but when we walk in truth while fulfilling our purpose, people will defiantly see that there is something unique and special about us. In John 1:4, it states that Jesus was the life and that the life was the light of men. The light shines in the darkness, but darkness doesn't understand. We see in John 1:23 that even though they didn't understand, they knew that John was special and even great in his calling.

When we have Jesus in our hearts, we not only have the truth that has the power to free men from their own minds, but that truth translated to Jesus's love and that empowers us to accomplish anything that God has called us to do. Many times, we as people think that love conquers all we do, and we find ourselves in situations like John did being imprisoned. Love conquers all that is empowered by truth and aligns with God's plan and purpose for our lives. When people questioned John's identity, he answered with Scripture because he knew who he was. The Word literally defined God's plan and purpose for His life. So as we start our day, let's take the time to read and apply God's Word to our lives. This will help us to understand who we are and the plan and purpose that God has for our lives. When we start our day in fellowship with our Creator, it sets the standard for the rest of our day.

Kim and I love you and are excited for all that God has in store for your life. Have a great day

Joy

The joy of the Lord is our strength! (Nehemiah. 8:10). So let's see what brings God joy? The Bible states that He delights in the man who trusts in Him and walks in obedience to the calling of God in our lives (Proverbs 8:30-31, Psalms 147:10-11, Proverbs 11:20). God delights in the righteous or those who are in right standing with Christ Jesus.

What else brings joy to the Lord? When we love people, lead others in truth and bring salvation to the lost and the dying. When we apply these principles, we empower others to walk in the fullness of God's provisions, giving them the same opportunities to disciple others.

When we are going through adverse situations, or Satan is attacking us, we need to keep in mind that the joy of the Lord is our strength. We should look for opportunities to bring God joy, because God's joy is our strength! God's promises are "yes" and "amen" (2 Corinthians 1:20) and no weapon formed against us will prosper (Isaiah 54:17). No matter what Satan uses to bring destruction in our lives, God will turn it around for His glory and our good! Serving God is a win-win situation. All things work together for our good because we love God and are called according to His purpose! (Romans 8:28).

Kim and I love you and are strengthened in knowing that as we encourage you in your faith, it brings joy to the Lord!

Enter God's Courts with Praise

The Bible states that God inhabits the praises of His people (Psalms 22:3). The significant aspect of this is God is light (1 John 1:5). Jesus stated He is the light of the world! (John 8:12).

Have you ever turned the light on? What happens? The dark disappears! That's because dark and light can't occupy the same space. Many of us deal with darkness in our lives such as depression, loss of hope, fear, and so on. That's why we need to read our Bibles (Proverbs 30:5, John 17:17). So that we can know the truth. Why? Because the truth will set us free! (John 8:32).

We need to learn how to praise God regardless of the darkness (John 1:5, John 12:46, 1 Thesselonians 5:18, Psalm 34). When God inhabits our praise, darkness has to go! Pretty cut and dried. That's why Satan always tries to separate us from God, implying that God is mad at us, or that we aren't good enough.

When darkness enters our lives, Satan is close by. The very thing that Satan wanted from the beginning was to be like God (Isaiah 14:13-15). Satan desired creation to turn to him, putting our focus on him rather than God. So put on your full armor of God, draw close to God, resist the devil and he will flee (Ephesians 6:10-18). Always remember God inhabits the praises of His people! (Psalms 22:3).

Kim and I love you and are excited for you in all that God is doing in you, threw you, and for you. Have a great day!

Enjoying Everyday Life

Learn to enjoy and trust God with your everyday life. Have you ever gotten up and had a list of things that you really needed to get accomplished, but something else came up and your entire day was put off? It is so easy to get upset, grumpy, and stressed because we can't accomplish what we needed to get done!

The good news is God is as interested in our everyday plans as He is in our happiness and His purpose for our lives! God reminds us of this in His Word: He states your footsteps are divinely ordered! (Psalms 37:23, Proverbs 20:24). If we take the time to trust that not only is God in control, but that wherever or whatever our day ends up to be, He has a purpose, and He has directed my footsteps for the day!

Don't allow a bad attitude or self-pity to rob you of your ability to enjoy the journey and fulfill your purpose for the day! As long as our focus is on ourselves and what we want, we can't be used by God to accomplish what He wants! (Ephesians 2:10, 2 Timothy 2:20-21). Every day, there are people in our lives, divine appointments, whom we have been given. If we will learn to trust God and know that when it's all God, it's all good, then we can effectively reach and be empowered to allow God's love, mercy, grace, and compassion to reach out and minister to those divine appointments that He placed in our lives! (Hebrews 13:1-2, 1 Corinthians 3:13, Psalms 119:73-80). It might be a kind word, a display of a good attitude, a kind gesture, a word of encouragement, or just a dis- play of God's peace in your life! Today is the day the Lord has made, rejoice and be glad in it! (Psalms 118:24). God's purpose is always greater than your plan!

Kim and I love you. Have a super awesome day!

Knowing Our Enemy

How can we be successful in our everyday lives? We first need to know who we are according to God's Word. Second, we need to know who our enemy is. What is Satan's mission? The Bible says that Satan is the father of lies and that he knows no truth! (John 8:44). Satan's only purpose is to steal, kill, and destroy (John 10:10).

Here is a food for thought. A thief only steals what is valuable! So what is it that Satan wants to steal, kill, and destroy? The Bible says that the kingdom of God is righteousness, joy, and peace! (Romans 14:17). This is everything that Jesus accomplished for us on the cross in a nutshell. Satan first wants to steal our righteousness, or our right standing with God. The second thing Satan wants to do is kill our joy. Why? The joy of the Lord is our strength (Nehemiah. 8:10). Last but not least, Satan wants to destroy our peace of mind in all that God has promised He would do in us, through us, and for us.

The good news in all of this is that Satan's only power over us is the power of suggestion. Satan knows no truth; in fact, God says that Satan is the father of lies. Satan might suggest that God is mad at us, but the truth is, God is mad about us. Satan might suggest that because we sin, we are no longer worthy of God's love. The truth is that if we are quick to repent of our sin, God is faithful to forgive us our sins (1 John 1:9). Always remember that Satan's suggestions are based on lies. It's only when we believe his lies that he gains access into our lives. Satan's goal is to keep us from running to God when we are in trouble, rather than running from God. Satan is like a man with no rope that is trying to convince us that we are tied up. *There is no rope!*

The meaning of true joy is this. Jesus first, others second, and yourself last. This kind of joy gives us the strength to accomplish all that God has for our lives. God's perfect plan for our lives is twofold. First, God wants to allow His love to flow through us so that all can experience salvation. Second, God wants us to experience all of His promises in our own lives. When we realize who we are in Christ and are walking in the fullness of whom God is, we are powerful and have no limitations of what God will do. Satan wants to convince us that we are pitiful. The truth is, we are powerful. Satan can't steal something unless we first possess it! We are righteous through Christ, we have strength through His joy, and we have peace that gives understanding of all that has been given to us. So let's stand up and fight for what is rightfully ours! Draw near to God, resist the devil, and he must flee.

Kim and I love you and pray that today you seek God and experience all that He has for your lives. Have a great day.

Labor in Rest

When we rest, God works and when we work, God rests! The Bible is pretty specific when instructing us to rest in the peace of God. Cast your cares on Him because He cares for you (1 Pet. 5:7). We are instructed not to worry about provision because not only does He take care of all creation but as Christians God provides our needs according to His riches (Philippians 4:19). When we begin to understand who we are in Christ due to our searching the Word of God, we can come to a place of complete peace because we understand that God is our all in all.

When we take matters into our own hands, we make messes and prolong the hand of God that works in our behalf. Why? God is a jealous God (Exod. 34:14). He doesn't want us doing anything but obeying His Word and trusting in Him. It is not our job to make a way, it's His job! God will not share the victory with anyone. Worry is a sin for a reason. When we worry, it's due to the fact that that we are no longer trusting God. God makes a way where there is no way (Philippians 2:13), He gives us favor with all the right people (Proverbs 3:4), He provides our needs, He vindicates us (Psalms 135:14), He is our protector (2 Thessalonians 3:3), our restorer (Psalms 51:10-12),

He is our all in all. When God is our everything, then His everything is available to us. When I lost my job, people said what will you do? I said, "God is my provider, and I am in covenant with Him, and I honor Him with my money." When I was hit by car and spent six months learning to walk again, I knew that my footsteps are divinely ordered and God was in control. When people have made false accusations regarding my character, I knew that my character is the character of Christ and that God is in control. God's Word is faithful, true, and just His promises are "yes" and "amen" (2 Corinthians 1:20), and He is not a man that He should lie. We can put our faith and trust in every word that comes from His mouth (Proverbs 30:5). When I stumble, I know that if I am quick to repent,

He is faithful to forgive. God's mercies are new every morning (Lamentations 3:22-23), and there is no condemnation in Christ (Romans 8:1). I am a child of God. He doesn't see my problems or shortcomings; He just sees my potential in Christ. When we know who we are in Christ, then no one or nothing can keep us from God's best. He will finish what He has started (Philippians 1:6). God has a plan and a purpose for each and every one of our lives and when we put our faith and trust in Him (Psalms 23). He causes us to walk by still waters and lay in green pastures; He fulfills our destiny in Him.

God states there are two reasons we as His people fail. The first is a lack of knowledge of His Word (Hosea 4:6). Second, not having vision (Proverbs 29:18). Vision can't be realized without the knowledge of God's Word. When we understand who we are in the Word and all that was made available to us, then we can have vision to fulfill our purpose in this earth. We can walk in peace knowing that God is in control and that our lives can be a representation or reflection of the fullness of God's greatness. The next time you feel the need to worry and help God, step back, take a deep breath, and know that when we let go and let God is all good.

Kim and I love you and are super excited to see you fulfill your purpose in Christ as you lead many to come to know and understand all that He has for them. Have a great day.

Let God Be Your GPS

If I were having a party at my house and you had never been to my house, I would give you the directions needed to arrive. How dumb would it be for you having never been to my house to argue my directions? If you were on your way to my house and made a wrong turn, you could call me and I would be more than willing to help get you back on track! How useless would it be to have an invitation to my party but no directions or address?

Jesus is the invitation to heaven or God's party. The Bible is the directions to effectively navigate you through life to reach the party victoriously! If you get lost along the way, all you have to do is call on God. God is the author and finisher of our faith (Hebrews 12:2). He helps to redirect our path bringing us back to right standing in Him!

Why is it that we often argue with God when it comes to instructions on how to live a victorious life? Who would say, "Oh I'm going to heaven, but I don't need directions"? The Bible stands for **B**asic **I**nstructions **B**efore **L**eaving **E**arth! God knows everything we need to be successful in this life, and He has made it available to us in His Word. The Bible states that God's Word is a lamp unto our feet (Psalms 119:105). It's through His Word that we can say my footsteps are divinely ordered!

The Word of God also gives us shoes of peace. The Bible didn't say everything would be candy and spice and all things nice. God said that He would provide us peace that would bring us through anything! One day, we will stand before God and He will ask us what we did with His Word. We have the potential for greatness and victory through His Word, or the potential for disaster without His Word! So if you are lost and unsure about which way to go, always remember God's mercies are new every morning (Lamentations 3:22-23). God is not mad at you; He is mad about you!

Kirk Ratliff

Kim and I love you and are excited for all that God is doing in you, through you, and for you!

Life or Death

I was in the store the other day and was looking at the Halloween items and had to chuckle. Again, there is a paradigm shift in the way Americans think. This year, we as a whole will spend a whopping nine billion dollars on Halloween paraphernalia. The Bible states that as a man thinks in his heart, so is he (Proverbs 23:7), and out of the abundance of the heart, the mouth speaks (Matthew 15:18). Halloween was once a holiday that honored the people who had passed in life. Today, it's about witches, ghouls, death, and anything related to hell.

When I saw a prop, which was a length of plastic chain, I was reminded of all that Jesus accomplished on the cross. Jesus was brutally murdered so that we could be made free. The chains of sin and death were broken as Jesus ascended into the bowels of hell, and He literally set the captives free (Romans 8:2). Two thousand years later, we decorate our homes and our children with every symbol of hell and death.

On the flip side, we as Americans have become bothered by people who embrace the true meaning of Christmas, and instead refer to Christmas as the winter holiday rather that the birth of the one who is the way, the truth, and the life. The Bible states that there will come a time when people will trade the truth of God for a lie while denying the power of God (Romans 1:25). Satan has an agenda, and the greatest scam he has ever accomplished was convincing us that, for one, he isn't real and second, that anything that has to do with death is just fun and make-believe. The truth is this. The Bible states that we have been presented with life or death, a blessing or a curse. Choose life (Deuteronomy 30:19).

Here are the lyrics to a popular rock song I thought would be appropriate for today's blog. All AC/DC:

Kirk Ratliff

I'm a rolling thunder, a pouring rain
I'm comin' on like a hurricane

My lightning's flashing across the sky
You're only young but you're gonna die

Won't take no prisoners, won't spare no lives
Nobody's putting up a fight

I got my bell, I'm gonna take you to hell
I'm gonna get you, Satan get you

Hells bells

Jesus is the Way, the Truth, and the Life, and no one comes to the Father except through him (John 14:6). God has an amazing plan and purpose for your life.

Kim and I love you. Have a great day!

Life without a Mirror

What is the significance in having a mirror? What would life be like if we didn't have any more mirrors? Can you imagine the bad hair day's people would have? What about you, ladies? What would it be like applying makeup with no mirror? I would imagine the chaos that would be experienced would be catastrophic! We often look in the mirror and rely on the reflection it gives us to make sure our image is good. We wouldn't be able to see if we had food on our shirt, our makeup was good, or we are shaved evenly!

The Word of God is a mirror for our spirit! (James 1:23). As we look into God's Word and read it, God begins to show us our imperfections and the things that we need to work on! The more that our spirit is in line with the Word of God, the clearer the reflection of who Jesus is in us and through us becomes!

Many times, people ask Jesus into their lives and their spirit gets born again, but they don't look into the mirror of God's Word! As we begin to seek God through His Word, then our intellect, will, and emotions begin to line up with what God has for our lives. This allows the spirit of God to shine in our lives, empowering us with His love to accomplish anything! It's when we get born again and don't look at ourselves in the mirror of the Word that we walk around in life stating that Jesus is in your heart, but there is no outward appearance of Him in your life. This only frustrates us because we think our quality of life should be better. The Word states we can have abundant life but because we don't know how to groom ourselves in the Word, our life remains a mess!

We have been given the ability to accomplish greatness. Jesus died a horrible death to pay the price for that abundant life. Don't go your whole life holding the Bible in your hands or placing it on a shelf. We can literally look into the Word and use it to refine who we are, allowing God's best to take root in our lives. Why? Well, for one, so we can live a life victoriously through any opposition that comes our way. The second reason is, so others can experience the power of

God's Word through us, allowing God's love to bring healing and freedom from sin and death. Most people spend years praying for the salvation of their loved ones when in reality, it's the love of God in us and through us that draws all to a place of salvation!

Kim and I love you and are excited to see you fulfill all that God has in store for you. Have a great day!

Love Conquers All

God states in His Word that He is love, and love conquers all. The Word states that Jesus is the Word made flesh. Jesus is in whole all that the Word is! So if God is love and a perfect representation of what the Word is, then love is the highest form or reflection of God in our lives. The Word states that perfect love cast out fear and conquers everything! (1 John 4:18). Wow!

So let's look at a couple character- istics of love! If love is the spirit of God, then the fruit of the spirit is such—love, joy, peace, patience, kindness, goodness, faithfulness, gentleness, and self-control, and against such, there are no laws! (Galatians 5:22-23). Why? Love is the fullness of God in us, the Fruit of the spirit!

Do you know someone in your life who works at displaying this kind of fruit in their lives? It's easy to be around them, and there is a particular sweetness about them that gives others the desire to be around them as well.

So here is the million-dollar question. How do we become the fullness of love? The Bible says be transformed by the renewing of our mind through the washing of the Word daily! (Romans 12:2). This means what? We need to read our Bible! If the Bible is the written word of God and Jesus was the Word made flesh then and we want to know God, then we need to read the book. When we are diligent in reading, then our minds eventually begin to think like God, allowing our lives to be a reflection of God. When the love of God flows through us, it will draw all people to know and understand God's love for them as well. We are able to share the plan of salvation with others, therefore, fulfilling our purpose in this life!

Kim and I love you and want great things for your life. Seek God and change the world as you know it. All through the faithful- ness of His love! Have a great day!

When Love Overcomes

Love is the highest form of spiritual warfare! Why? True love conquers all (1 Corinthians 13). So what is true love? God is true love. We often see love as a mushy, girly, chick flick kind of thing. True love has the ability to bring grown men to a place of literally being lethal in the kingdom of heaven. True love is hard but has amazing results. True love forgives when we have a right to hate. Love prays for and has compassion on a person's soul, even when that person has lied, used, and stolen from us.

True love is not easy, but it literally sets us up for greatness. It was Christ's love that while beaten, bleeding, convulsing with pain, and just minutes from death, said, "Forgive them for they don't know what they are doing" (Luke 23:34). His love was more concerned about their soul than the pain they had inflicted on Him. How do we gain the power of love in our lives?

The Bible says that Jesus is God and God is love (John 1:1). God's Word also states that the Word of God or the Bible is Jesus in written form (John 1:14). The more we read and apply the Word in our hearts, the greater the reflection of Jesus we possess. The more love we are equipped with, the more powerful we become. That's why we can do all things through Christ because He is love, and love conquers all (Philippians 4:13). This is the atomic bomb of spiritual warfare.

Do you have what it takes to be a great warrior? It's the love of God through us that draws all people to a place of understanding their destiny in Christ (Romans 2:4). When love guides us, we are unstoppable in what God can do in us, through us, and for us. Let's choose this day who we will serve! There are souls depending on us. We can be the light in a dark place that brings hope and freedom to the lost and the dying.

Kim and I love you. Go and change the world as you see it, one act of love at a time!

Don't Be Fooled by a Counterfeit

Every good thing that God has for us, Satan has a counterfeit to offer. *Webster's* dictionary defines counterfeit as, "something made in the imitation of something else with the intent to deceive."

The Bible says that God's people perish for a lack of vision (Proverbs 29:18). So what is vision? The act or power to perceive something in your imagination. So let's look at why it's so important to have vision of what could be. The Bible states that through Christ, I can do all things (Philippians 4:13). So vision has no boundaries. God literally empowers us for greatness. What is the purpose to this unlimited ability? To reach the lost and the dying, leading them to a place of understanding of all that Jesus accomplished for them.

So let's look at the counterfeit, the negative side of vision. The Bible states that as man thinks, so is he (Proverbs 23:7). Some use their imagination for perversion, which leads to wrong relationships, STDs, divorce, and in some cases, prison. Vision in Christ gives us freedom and the impossible. Imagination in Satan or sin leads to hopelessness and bondage! When you use your imagination, even for wealth and prosperity outside of God's plan and purpose, it always leads to death.

Jesus stated that many will stand before him claiming great accomplishments (Matthew 7:21- 23). He will say depart from me for I never knew you! Why? Because we only receive credit when Jesus is the center of our journey. The journey of the cross is twofold. First, it is for our salvation. Once we are born again, then vision comes to play. Second, God empowers us to lead others to the cross. No matter what your vision is, use every opportunity to advance the gospel.

The greatest commodity on the earth is a soul, and the only thing on this earth that we can take to heaven is another soul. We need to live our lives on purpose and with purpose. Allow yourselves to dream big, and God will use you to change the world as you know it! God has an amazing plan and purpose for our lives. Seek God and experience unlimited potential in His greatness!

Kim and I love you and are super excited to see you fulfill your purpose. Have a great day!

D.R.A.M.A.

<u>D</u>eep <u>R</u>ooted <u>A</u>ttaching <u>M</u>ental <u>A</u>nguish! Drama is always contrary to the Word of God and can only manifest when we as Christians don't take our thoughts captive while walking in the overcoming power of God's Word. When someone surrounds themselves with drama, they tend to become emotional vampires, sucking the life and peace out of our lives. The Word of God removes all uncertainties of what could be, what might be, what should've been, and so forth.

Satan always wants to cause mental anguish, because he knows it robs us of our peace. Peace is a vital part of our armor as a Christian. It's the shoes of peace that take us down the path of righteousness and protect our feet from stumbling. Knowing who you are in Christ will give you the confidence of His peace in every area of your life. There is never a place for drama in a Christian's life! Jesus is the prince of peace, and if Jesus lives inside us, then peace should also reside in us.

The Bible states that all things good or bad work together for our good and His glory (Romans 8:28). Drama keeps us from having clarity and experiencing God's faithfulness! So drop the drama, put your faith and trust in Jesus, and know that when it's all God, it's all good!

Kim and I love you. Have a great day!

Love Is Not an Experience – It's a Lifestyle

Salvation frees us from a limited way of thinking and gives us the ability to think like God. The Bibles states that man's thoughts are not God's thoughts, and man's ways are not God's ways (Isaiah 55:8). When we ask Jesus into our hearts, we have the opportunity to seek God through reading and applying His Word to our lives. When we educate ourselves in God's Word, it literally gives us the ability to think like God. The Bible states that as a man thinks, so is he (Proverbs 23:7), and out of the abundance of the heart, the mouth speaks (Matthew 15:8). So when we think like God, we speak like God, and our lives are literally a reflection of who God is. The purpose of thinking properly is, it helps us to understand what true love is.

The Bible states that there is no greater love than someone who will lay his life down for another (John 15:13). So how do we do this? The Bible gives us many ways to apply this to our lives. An example of this would be to bless those who curse you (Matthew 5:44). We can do this by praying and speaking kind words to them and about them. The Bible states that the power of life or death is in our tongue (Proverbs 18:21). Think about this, Jesus is the Way, the Truth, and the Life (John 14:6). When we know God's Word and we speak a blessing, we are literally bringing life or Jesus to the issue. In the book of John, it states that in the beginning was the Word, the Word with God, and the Word was God. In the book of Matthew, it states that Jesus is the Word made flesh. So if Jesus is God and God is love and love conquers all, then when we speak life, we are empowered by love, and no weapon formed against can or will prosper.

The more we understand who God is and what He desires for our lives, the deeper His love takes root inside us, the more powerful we become. Jesus is our rock and when we build our house on Him, the storms of life will never move us because Jesus is love, and love conquers all (Matthew 7:24- 27). As we learn to live our lives according to the Word of God, we understand and are empowered to live our lives on purpose, and we are empowered to accomplish anything because Jesus is our strength. Stop looking at love as an experience and learn to be a reflection of God's love. Love is empowered by truth, and truth sets the captives free (Luke 4:18). Free from what? The old way of thinking and doing. The Bible states that in and of ourselves, the way we think and the things we do, we can accomplish nothing. But when we say yes to God's way of thinking and doing, then the sky is the limit. To infinity and beyond! When we become the love of God, then we are literally empowered by His love daily.

Kim and I love you and are excited for all that God is doing in you, through you, and for you. Have a great day

Love vs. Promise

Sometimes, as Christians, we confuse God's love with His promises! God's love is eternal and unconditional, meaning we can't earn it; we can't lose it; His love for you will always be, regardless! Even when a man walks away from God and chooses to spend eternity in hell, God still loves him! But the promises are not unconditional. Yes, Jesus died so that we can be saved and that all of His promises are available to us, but in order to walk in victory, you have to do your part! For example, if I hire you to work for my firm, I set a standard of what is expected of you and your success depends on doing your part and in return, I pay your salary. It would be foolish of you to think that you are entitled a paycheck if you didn't do what is required of you!

In the same way, God requires you to do your part and in return, He will guarantee His promises! For example, God's Word states that He will prosper in everything we put our hands to do, but it requires us to put our hands to doing something (Deuteronomy 30:9). If you are expecting financial return, you have to first honor God with your tithe and offering. God states that the tithe stops the hand of the devourer from taking what you have (Malachi 3:11); opens the windows of heaven to pour out a blessing you can't contain! (Malachi 3:10). Jesus stated He is the vine and we are the branches, and if we will abide in Him by reading and applying the Word of God in our lives, then we will bear fruit, meaning the promises will work because we have done our part and we will reflect the goodness of God in our lives! (John 15:5).

Jesus went on to say that if we do not produce fruit of the Word in our lives, then we are not in Him, and we will wither and die and be thrown in the fire! The beauty of good fruit is, it is not only appealing to others, but it also brings spiritual nourishment to those who eat of it! The fruit brings God's blessings to your life, and it also teaches others how to cultivate their own fruit! So read your Bible, apply what it says, and watch God do amazing things in your life. In Him, you are empowered by limitless opportunities, because in Him, we can do anything!

Kim and I love you and are excited about God's plan and pur- pose for you. Have a great day!

Making a Difference

I have been pretty busy the past few days and haven't taken the time to sit down and write an inspirational. I received a text this morning stating that my words of inspiration were missed. The texter went on to ask if I would take a minute to seek God for today's encouraging word.

It's important for all of us to take time away from the hustle and bustle of our busy lives to realize that others are able to see Jesus in us, and our lives do make a difference. We live in uncertain times bombarded with negativity and the what ifs that life sometimes offers. When we can bring encouragement to this lost and dying world, it's like a ray of hope to some and a breath of fresh air to others.

The Bible states that iron sharpens iron (Proverbs 27:17). I may be strong in the area that you are weak, and you might be strong in the area that I am weak. When we allow God to work through us, we literally sharpen each other. There are people in your circle of life whom I may never know or have access to. When we help strengthen and encourage each other, we are empowered to reach and encourage all. We are now reaching a multitude together and accomplishing the great commission. The Word educates us, love empowers us, and the result is good, desirable, life-changing fruit.

Kim and I love you guys and are always excited to know God is fulfilling His plan and purpose in your lives. Have a super awesome day.

New Beginnings

Today is a new day, and God's mercies are new every morning (Lamentations 3:22-23). Yesterday is gone and the slate is clean, so don't live in the past wasting time on the should've, would've, or could've done! The Bible states that we can do all things through Christ because He is our strength (Philippians 4:13). Stop saying I can't, and quit living in the past. The Bible states that a man who puts his hand to the plow but yet looks back is unworthy of the kingdom, meaning you can'teffectively move forward while looking backwards! (Luke 9:62).

Always remember, God states that our footsteps are divinely ordered (Psalms 37:23). Don't worry about where you are or complain about your current situation. Learn to enjoy the journey and know that God is in control! That's why the Bible states do all things without grumbling or complaining (Philippians 2:14). When we complain, it only breeds more of what we don't want. When we have a thankful heart, it gives God the ability to work in our behalf!

I was talking to a friend the other day and he is not happy with his current job. He makes great money but is never home to see his family. I asked him if he ever prayed about it, he stated, "No not really." I reminded him that God's Word says seek first the kingdom and everything else will be added to us (Matthew 6:33). We often seek everything else and then want to try and fit God into our mess. Learn to trust God, live your life for Him, and realize that everything God has for us gives us purpose! Live your life knowing that your willingness to serve God just might be a purpose for someone else's life!

Kim and I love you. Have a great day!

The Only Thing Keeping Us from God's Best Is Us

When God delivered Israel from four hundred years of slavery, they were faced with great opposition. Have you ever wondered why God just doesn't bring what you need? Opposition causes us to either trust or run. Character is built not by what we go through but how we handle what we go through. The Word of God empowers us not only to overcome adversity, but to experience the faithfulness of God's amazing provision as well. God had not only promised to deliver His people out of their bondage, but also gave them hope of a promised land flowing with milk and honey (Isaiah 43). The problem is, they never truly allowed adversity to build the character they needed to enjoy not only God's provision, but the journey that would take them to the promised land. Every time adversity would come, they would grumble and complain rather than embracing the adversity and trusting that God was in control. God had not brought them out of bondage to watch them fail. God wanted them to trust Him in the opposition in order to embrace the final promise of a land flowing with milk and honey (Romans 8:12-17). A couple million people were delivered from Egypt's oppression. When it came time for them to experience the promised land, they sent out twelve spies to check out the land. When the spies returned, ten of them said that there were giants in the land, and it was just too dangerous. The other two talked of God's great provision in the land.

God will never give us a vision for purpose in our lives without also providing the provision necessary to experience the fullness of that dream or vision for our lives. God has not given us a spirit of fear (2 Timothy 1:7). When we learn to put our faith and trust in God's ability rather than our own strength, or the size of the problem, then and only then will we enjoy the fruit of His provision. Then we cannot only enjoy the journey, but also experience the beauty of His plan and provision for our lives. When we complain, we remain to go through opposition over and over without getting anywhere. The Israelites went around the mountain for forty years because they refused to trust God and quit complaining (Numbers 14:26-38). The trip that was only supposed to take eleven days took forty years!

The only thing keeping us from experiencing all that God has for us is us. Read your Bible, apply it to your life, put your trust in God, and know that when we let go and let God, it's all good. Learn to enjoy the journey, God is in control, and our footsteps are divinely ordered! (Psalms 37:23-24, Proverbs 20:24).

Kim and I love you. Have a great day.

No Greater Love

The Bible states that the love of God conquers all! (1 Corinthians 13). Jesus is perfect love and lives in us. This is why the Bible states that the love of God through us draws all to know and understand the saving grace of Jesus Christ (Romans 2:4).

Why is giving the highest form of worship? Because when we give in love, we are a perfect reflection of God's image. Why? God was the first to give (1 Peter 1:20). God gave His son to us through love and because of this, we were drawn to and experienced salvation along with the fullness of all that God is and desires for our lives.

When we go to work, we trade our time for the company's money, resulting in a paycheck. That paycheck is our life! We trade forty hours of our lives and in return, we receive money for our time. The Bible says that there is no greater love than someone who will lay their lives down for another (John 15:13). When we honor God with our finances while advancing the gospel, we are literally laying our lives down for someone else to experience the fullness of God's plan and purpose for their lives. When we give by faith and fuelled by His love through us, we are unstoppable. The Bible states that we can do all things through Christ because He is our strength (Philippians 4:13). When we pray according to God's Word concerning His will in giving, the Bible states that God not only hears our prayers but He also answers them (1 John 5:14). This is an example of a powerful prayer based on the Word of God.

> Father God, I thank you that my life belongs to you and because of your love and your giving, I have been set free and made whole because of all that Jesus accomplished on the cross. I thank you that I have been created in your image, and as I lay my life down and give with your love, many will come to know and understand your love, mercy, grace, and compassion. Thank you for all that you are doing in me, through me, and for me in Jesus's name. Amen.

The Simplicity of a Practical Jesus

This is a prayer of faith. Faith comes from the Word of God (Romans 10:17). When we pray by faith according to God's Word and allow His love to empower us, we are literally unstoppable. Always remember that when our hands are closed, we stop the flow of God's provision. If God can't get it through us, He can't get it to us. Let's seek God this week by reading and applying His Word to our lives. God has an amazing plan for our lives.

Kim and I love you and are excited to see you flourish in God's greatness. Have a great day!

Walking in Faith

What pleases God? A man who lives a life of faith! Faith is not the random belief that something can and will happen, but rather true faith is empowered by the Word of God. The Bible states that Jesus is the Word made flesh (John 1:14). Every promise and every provision that is in the Word is exactly who Jesus is. That's why through Christ, I can do all things (Philippians 4:13).

I am empowered to walk in faith, as I am diligent to read and apply all that the Word says is mine. I have hope that not only is God's Word true, but it will also accomplish everything it states it will do. The Bible states that faith comes from hearing the Word of God (Romans 10:17). So if we lack faith in a certain area or is unsure of what God has to say regarding a situation in your life, then pick up the book and seek Him out! The Word states that we can do *all* things because Christ is our strength! This is a lifestyle with no boundaries as for what God can and will do in you, through you, and for you.

Don't hear what I'm not saying. I am not saying that if you don't read your Bible, then God will be mad or disappointed with you! His love for us is eternal and regardless of anything we could say, think, or do, He will always love us. When we don't read and apply His Word, we won't ever know the satisfaction of living the life of an overcomer!

God loves you more than you know and you are the apple of His eye (Zechariah 2:8). When we grow in His Word and learn to accomplish great things in our lives, God is like a proud parent super excited, just as we are when our children succeed in life. The sky is the limit; dream big, stretch your faith, and watch God take your ordi- nary and turn it into His extraordinary, and make all things possible!

Kim and I love you and are excited to see you accomplish all that God has in store for your life. Have a great day!

No Guilt in Jesus

The truth will set you free! (John 8:32). Free from what? The plans and schemes of the enemy giving us victory over Satan! There is power in the Word of God (1 Corinthians 4:20, 2 Timothy 3:16-17). The Word is truth and when applied brings truth in our lives. The last couple of days, I have been struggling with stupid actions on my part and feeling very defeated and guilty.

I have made decisions that are contrary to what I know is good for my life! Have you ever heard someone use the term making a mountain out of a molehill? Sin is nothing more than a molehill. Why? Because we are all going to make mistakes; it's part of our human nature. God's Word states that a righteous man falls seven times, but he gets back up (Proverbs 24:16).

Jesus paid the price for our sins past, present, and future! The enemy comes and uses guilt along with feelings of failure to keep us from experiencing the truth that gives us freedom from sin and death. He takes our molehill and talks us into seeing a mountain! Satan's greatest scheme is the power of suggestion! The Bible states draw near to God, resist the devil and he will flee! (James 4:7). God continues to encourage us by stating that His mercies are new every morning! (Lamentations 3:22-23).

When we confess our sins, God is faithful and just to forgive us our sins! (1 John 1:9). And think about this, God states in His Word that when He forgives us, our sins are cast into the sea of forgetfulness, never to be remembered again! (Isaiah 43:25, Hebrews 8:12). So we truly may fall seven times, but if we confess as soon as we fall, it's immediately forgiven and forgotten. In reality, you are always on your first offense and seven never comes! God gives us His grace, mercy, and compassion and wants nothing but success for our lives

Don't fall for Satan's suggestions of failure and guilt. Don't allow Satan's suggestions to turn your molehill into a mountain. Choose to walk in the forgiveness and the mercy that has been made available to you through all that Jesus accomplished on the cross!

Kim and I love and are excited for all that God has in store for your life. Have a great day!

Not by What We See

When we allow circumstance to rob us of our faithfulness! Faithfulness to serve and seek God in our lives is a decision based on necessity because in and of ourselves, we can do nothing (2 Corinthians 3:5). Life without God is hopeless, hard, and always in crisis. Sometimes, we as people have adversity in our lives. We allow the plans and schemes of Satan to keep us from seeking God. In reality, that's when we should be the closest to God.

Don't think that there will ever be a good time to serve God. The enemy will always make sure there is something or someone who will deter us from the things of God. We shouldn't rely on prayer lines and prayer teams to be our connection to God. These things can only do so much for us. When it comes down to it, the proof is in the pudding. Success is what we do or don't do that matters. We need to read our Bibles, refresh our minds, build our faith, and learn to fight the good fight.

Why be pitiful when we have the potential to be powerful? Remember it's through Christ that we can accomplish anything! (Philippians 4:13). So do what you know you need to do. We need to cultivate a relationship with Jesus, make Him top priority in our lives, renew our mind daily by reading our Bibles, and allow God to transform our pitiful into His powerful!

Kim and I love you. Have a great day!

Nothing More Than Feelings

The side effects of feelings! The world as we know it doesn't have the answers needed to offer complete mental stability with or without medication. I know so many people who are heavily medicated for anxieties and are no more stable than when they started taking meds. Kim and I have counseled many people watching them get totally free from the wrong feelings that controlled their lives and without any medications whatsoever! How is this possible?

The Word of God is so amazing. It offers peace of mind, stability in an unstable world; it calms the anxious, it overcomes fear and depression (1 Pet. 5:7, Philippians 4:7). God's Word sets the mentally captive free (2 Corinthians 3:17, 2 Timothy 1:7). How is this possible and why aren't more people experiencing this type of freedom? The Word of God offers all the stability we need but requires that we put our lives, our faith, and trust in the truth it provides (James 2:14). When feelings arise that are contrary to God's truths, we learn to take those thoughts captive, pulling down the strong holds that Satan uses to imprison us in our minds (2 Corinthians 10:4).

Over the last year, I have counseled three different people on multiple medications for anxieties, fears, and depression. The Word of God is so faithful that these people are not only stable but also free from any and all meds. The reason most people choose the meds over the Word of God is because it's easier to pop a pill than work the Word of God. Please don't hear what I'm not saying. I'm not saying to just ditch your meds; however, I am saying seek God's healing through His Word while enjoying the benefits of a sound mind. God's Word states that He has not given us a Spirit of fear but of a sound mind (2 Timothy 1:7).

You might ask how do I know that I too can have and experience that type of healing? God isn't a respecter of persons. What He does for one, He will do for all! (Acts 10:34). When Jesus died on the cross, He wore a crown of thorns. Because Jesus bled from His head, it was to provide healing in our minds. We don't have to continue living a life imprisoned by the feelings that control our minds.

Kim and I love you and want God's best for you. Have a great day.

The Potential of Seeds

The potential of greatness is deposited in us on the day we ask Jesus into our hearts. God literally plants seeds of love, joy, peace, patience, kindness, gentleness, and self-control. These are the seeds that when cultivated will bring the fullness of all that God wants to be in our lives. I can have an apple seed, and I can have a green thumb, but if I never plant that apple seed, I will never see its full potential. I will never be able to bite into a ripe juicy apple, I can never bake an apple crisp, and I will never be able to offer the benefit of its nourishment to others. All of the seeds' potential is dependent on my willingness to plant the seed. The process doesn't stop there. I need to water and provide care for the seed from bugs and other circumstances that would try to destroy the potential for a great harvest. During the growth process, there are many different problems that come along that try to keep my harvest from manifesting.

The same process applies to our spiritual life as well. Always remember that my natural life, what I see, taste, hear, smell, and feel are all a result of my spiritual life. What you see in the natural started in the spiritual, just as a mature apple tree started as a seed. Remember, the Bible states that as a man thinks, so is he! (Proverbs 23:7). When we learn to think like God, then we experience God's best in our lives. When we begin to read our Bibles, educating ourselves with the knowledge of God, we are literally empowered to cultivate the seeds of the fruit of the spirit in our lives. The foundation for all things in life is the ability to love. Why? Because love has the ability to conquer anything and everything.

As we cultivate a red hot love walk with God by reading and applying His Word, our lives become a reflection of God's love. The Bible states that the love of God through us draws all to a place of understanding of who God is and all that He has for our lives (Romans 2:4). We will always need to cultivate the seeds that produce the fruit of the spirit. The joy of the Lord is our strength and gives us the stamina to cultivate our other seeds (Nehemiah. 8:10).

The Simplicity of a Practical Jesus

When we walk in love powered by joy, it gives birth to peace and in return, peace helps us understand the nature of God and all that He wants in our lives. The next few seeds defiantly require willingness and a good work ethic on our behalf.

The Bible states that faith without works is dead (James 2:14-26). So the first seeds we plant are seeds of faith: love, joy, and peace; the second half of our seeds require works: patience, kindness, gentleness, and self-control. When we combine faith with works, it produces the most beautiful crop and gives us the opportunity to experience the fullness of God and all that He desires for our lives. His desire is for us to take this fruit and give it to others as an amazing reflection of God's faithfulness. This empowers us to change the world one soul at a time. Always remember that we can never have or experience anything good without first doing our part.

God's Word is true, faithful, and just (Psalms 33:4, Revelation 22:6). His promises are "yes" and "amen" (2 Corinthians 1:20), and His love endures forever (Psalms 100:5). When we say yes to God's ways and no to our old way of thinking, God takes our ordinary and empowers it with His extra, making our lives extraordinary! Always remember that a healthy apple tree doesn't have to convince people of the legitimacy. The fruit is the legitimacy of the tree. We don't have to sell people on our Christianity. Our fruit is the proof of who we are in Christ.

Kim and I love you and are excited for you to experience the fruit of God's grace and His faithfulness. Have a great day.

The Pot of Gold at the End of the Rainbow

Have you ever considered what the rainbow is? The rainbow is a promise of God and a reflection of God's faithfulness. What is the gold at the end of the rainbow? The manifestation of God's promises and the fulfillment of His purpose in our lives.

The Bible states that there are two reasons that God's people fail (Hosea 4:6, Proverbs 29:18). Wow, only two! To think that when there is a possibility of millions of reasons, there are only two! The first being a lack of knowledge of God's word, and second, a lack of vision or purpose in our lives.

We can never realize our purpose if we have no knowledge of His Word. The Word is the fuel that empowers us as God's people not only to have purpose, but also to fulfill His purpose in our lives. Have you ever met someone and every time you saw them, they have a new adventure or purpose? They are excited about what God wants to do in their lives, but they never accomplish or finish the last adventure or plan that allows purpose to flourish in their lives. These people often go their whole lives and never experience the finished plan that God has for them. Their only experience is, hope deferred which makes the heart sick. Why? When we believe in what we think God wants to do in us, through us, and for us, but never experience the satisfaction of seeing something completed, we are often discouraged, giving birth to confusion as to why things seem to never work out.

The reason that many are called, but few are chosen, is because most people want God's best, and they want to be used by God to accomplish greatness in this life, but when the rubber meets the road, they are not willing to stick with and apply God's Word to see the finished product of purpose. Fulfilling our destiny in Christ not only takes gifts and abilities, but it also requires dedication and discipline to the instruction of God's Word. Ninety percent of Christians say they are just waiting on God to make the dream happen.

The Simplicity of a Practical Jesus

The truth is, God is waiting for us to submit to His Word with a willing heart to do whatever He asks us to do. Most people never see the dream come true because they are not willing to do what God asks. Many times, we see what God is doing in other people's lives, and we want what they have but are not willing to do what they did in order to get what they have. The rainbow is a reflection of God's promise, the pot of gold is the fullness of God's provision (Genesis 9:13). If God calls us to do something, He will always provide the provision for the vision. When the prodigal son sought His father's provision, it took him to a place that left him broke, busted, and disgusted (Luke 15:11-32). It wasn't until he sought His father's heart that he was celebrated and restored to fulfill the purpose He was created for. Stop seeking provision. Provision is the result of God's faithfulness and our willingness to seek God's heart.

Kim and I love you and want to see you fulfill your purpose in Christ while changing the world, accomplishing the impossible, and reaching the lost and the dying. All because God is your strength. Have a great day!

The Power of Prayer

Kim and I went to breakfast in our little town at the local bar. We sat down and couldn't help but to watch as the locals came in for their Saturday routine of breakfast, coffee, and reading the morning paper. While we were watching, in walked a skinny man unkempt and looking rough from a Friday night of drinking. With him was this beautiful little girl probably ten-ish. He was very hateful to her and verbally abusive. He was using profanity and just bullying her, telling her she wasn't like normal children and that she was nothing more than a little liar. As we listened more, she was living with her grandma, and this was a weekend at Dad's. The little girl responded in a beat down voice, "What did I do, Daddy?" I almost cried, my heart was breaking because I just knew this was not a one-time ordeal. Her self-esteem was damaged already at her tender age.

The Bible says that we have authority over all principles and powers of darkness and whatever we bind on earth is bound in heaven (Luke 10:19, Matthew 18:18). Kim and I began to pray to ourselves very quietly, using the authority that was made available to us through all that Jesus accom- plished on the cross. I prayed:

> Father God, thank you for your love, your mercy, and your compassion. I bind this spirit of anger, rage, and resentment off of this man, and I lose him to receive from your ministering angels and your Holy Spirit. I come against any and all plans and schemes of Satan that would try and steal this little girl's hope of knowing love, in Jesus's name, amen.

As we sat there waiting for our meal, this man's entire demeanor changed. He was soft spoken, loving, and having a daddy/baby girl moment. He was stroking her hair and listening intently to her adventures of her hay ride the night before. She was excited to tell her daddy all about it. The hatefulness was gone, and the spirit of God was at work. I couldn't keep a dry eye, as I looked across the table at Kim, she also had tears in her eyes. As we held hands, we just said, "Thank you, Jesus!" The power of prayer! The Word of God is amazing, and because we read our Bibles, we were equipped to pray an effective prayer that was able to take a horrible situation and turn it into a beautiful one. God is not a respecter of persons, what He did for us today, He desires to do through all of you as well (Acts 10:34). His Word is amazing and His promises are "yes" and "amen" (2 Corinthians 1:20). Seek God in His Word daily and take His love to the world and make a difference.

Kim and I love you and are super excited about what God is doing in you, through you, and for you! Have a great day!

O.B.E.D.I.E.N.C.E

O: *Obedience*. When we hear the word obedience, we often think of discipline. I mean, after all, if I don't do what is required, then I'm subject to consequence. But the reality is that obedience is a gift and a privilege. It's a key that unlocks all that God has for us. It literally makes all things possible in our lives.

B: *Benefit*. Every promise that God gives us in His Word is attached to a command. There are 3,573 promises in the Bible, and each one of them is for our benefit but are only available through our willingness to do what is required of us.

E: *Eternal*. God's promises are "yes" and "amen" (2 Corinthians 1:20). His Word is eternal, and He watches over His Word to perform it and when we apply His Word, it will always accomplish what it was sent to do (Jeremiah 1:12). But faith without works is dead (James 2:14-26). God always requires us to do our part.

D: *Dedicated*. When I dedicate my life to applying the Word of God to my life, it literally becomes a lamp unto my path. Lighting the way so that my footsteps can be divinely ordered. Not only is the light giving me direction, but it's illuminating my heart, allowing the love of God to flow freely from my life drawing all to know and understand the saving grace of Jesus Christ.

I: *Inventory*. If we will take inventory every day of our lives and making sure that our lives are truly a reflection of all that Jesus is, then our lives are free from pitfalls that the enemy throws out for us trying to keep us from God's best.

E: *Excellence*. When we live an intentional life loving God and intentionally living a life of obedience, the Bible states that God seeks throughout the earth for a faithful heart He can bless (2 Chronicles 16:9). It's never for less, it's always for more! If God is asking you to give something up, it's because He has something better for you.

The Simplicity of a Practical Jesus

N: *Nothing.* No weapon formed against us will prosper (Isaiah 54:17), and nothing is impossible (Philippians 4:13) because in Christ, I can do all things. Obedience literally empowers us for greatness. The Bible states that even when Satan comes against us, if we will draw close to God staying focused on Him, then even adversity turns into opportunity for our benefit.

C: *Calling.* It's not God's desire that any man should perish but that all have eternal life (2 Pet. 3:9). All are called to greatness; unfortunately, few are chosen due to their unwillingness to bow their knee to God's will for their lives (Matthew 22:14).

E: *Endless.* God's mercies, His promises, His love are eternal; they are the first and the last the begging and the end they will never fade away they will always be. That is comforting for me because I know that as I seek God that His endless goodness is mine and His love, mercy, and compassion are the very things that guide and protect me and give me every good thing. God loves you and wants amazing things for your life. Will you allow Jesus in your heart and dedicate your life in obedience for all that He asks of you in His Word? Don't just be called, be chosen.

Kim and I love you. Have a great day.

One Way or the Other

God's way versus your way! This is a true story. It is about two persons who both have Jesus in their hearts. The difference is one understands who they are in Christ, and the other one doesn't. One reads his or her Bible and spends time seeking God's will for his or her life, and the other one doesn't! Two people both saved and going to heaven, but only one will live in God's peace and provision; the other will not.

The first person seeks God's direction in every area of his or her life and although he or she is not perfect, God's provision is evident in his or her life. Both people work for the same company and started at the same time making the same money. One honors God with their money; the other one does not. One looks at the job as a go-nowhere kind of job and tolerates the job as a hardship with no hope in sight of promotion or advancement. The other person knows that although they make minimum wage that God is their source and the sky is the limit. Six months later, one quits because, after all, each one they work with says, "This job sucks and, well, this is as good as it gets." The other does his or her job as unto the Lord and is promoted with a huge increase and full benefits.

The moral of the story is this, God is not a respecter of persons (Acts 10:34); He wants to bless and provide for all of His people the difference is one allowed the job and other employees to decide their future and one allowed God to guide their future. With God, all things are possible; seek His wisdom and direction through reading and applying His Word (Matthew 19:26). God says His Word is a lamp unto our feet, and our footsteps are divinely ordered when we seek His way (Psalms 119:105).

Kim and I love you. Have a great day.

Opposition Is the New Opportunity

Many times in our lives, we look at opposition as a downer or a negative. Opposition can be a huge positive if we see it for what it really is. Opposition is a tactic of Satan to keep us from fulfilling our purpose and potential while walking in the power of God's amazing word.

The Bible states that God's mercies are new every morning (Lamentations 3:22-23). We also know that if we are truly cleaning the slate daily, then God has no record of yesterday. The Bible states that when God forgives, He throws our sin in the sea of forgetfulness never to be remembered again (Mic. 7:19). The only reason Satan is adamant to throw opposition our direction is because he not only sees our potential but he knows that in Christ, we can do all things (Philippians 4:13). Opposition is nothing more than a smoke screen that is meant to redirect our focus of the problem away from the answer, exposing the opportunity for greatness.

God has an amazing plan and purpose for all of our lives (Jeremiah 29:11). God wants to do the impossible not only for us but through us. When our lives become a reflection of God's Word, and we are familiar with God's promises and fully aware of whom we are in Christ, then we are literally unstoppable! Joseph is a perfect example of not only God's plan, but His purpose as well. Joseph stayed the course; he never lost his identity in God. Joseph was faithful regardless the opposition and as a result, he became not only the second in control of all of Egypt, but he saved thousands of lives as well.

We can never reach our potential if all we can see is the opposition. Always remember that today is a new day, God's promises are "yes" and "amen:; His Word is faithful, true, and just, and His love through us can accomplish anything. God has provided all that is needed for us to live a life of victory. Opposition is nothing more than an elaborate lie of Satan to try and keep us from our potential in Christ. Always remember that when we are fulfilling our purpose, we are reaching our potential and lives are being impacted for the greater good of the gospel.

Kim and I love you and are cheering for you. Have a great day.

Our Footsteps Are Divinely Ordered

The hardest part about serving God is getting past ourselves. When life happens and things don't seem to work the way we think they should, we tend to get offended, hurt, mad, disappointed, and discouraged. The whole point of reading and applying the Word of God to our lives is that when life presents the opportunities to experience these feelings, we are able to process them properly and walk in all that God's Word offers, while trusting that God's plan is never for less but always for more. When we learn who we are in Christ and all that is available to us because of what Jesus accomplished on the cross, then trusting is the key that gives us freedom from our own wants, desires, and feelings.

Kim and I are once again faced with some changes in our lives. Our first response was feeling discouraged because the circumstances feel personal. In reality, God is in control (Joshua 1:9). God will never leave us or forsake us (Hebrews 13:5). His Word is faithful, true, and just. His promises are "yes" and "amen" (2 Corinthians 1:20). He watches over His Word to perform it, and anything Satan intended for harm, God will reverses Satan's actions for His glory and our benefit. Faith is nothing more than trusting that God is who He says He is and that He will do what He has promised to do. When we trust in what we don't see, it empowers the unseen to be seen.

This is faith in a nutshell; God said it, I believe it, therefore, I will see it. Do we always know every detail to what God has in store for us? No! But we do know that as long as we seek God and put our faith and trust in Him, we will see the fullness of all that He is and has for our lives. God wants great things for our lives and has gone to great lengths to ensure that we can have all that He promises. So as opposition presents itself, let's take the focus off ourselves and place it on God's faithfulness. This takes us from a victim mentality and makes us more than a conqueror. Let's read our Bible and seek God in all we do, say, and think, and rest in knowing that He is in control.

Kirk Ratliff

Kim and I love you, have a great day.

Our Potential

Love never sees the problem, it only sees the potential. The Bible says that God is love, and love conquers all! (1 John 4:8; 1 Corinthians 13). Jesus made the most powerful statement as He died on the cross, "It is finished!" What is finished? The problem, sin! One of the biggest problems in the body of Christ is we look at a person's problems and disqualify them in reaching their full potential in Christ Jesus. The whole purpose of what Jesus did on the cross was to eliminate the problem and pre-qualify everyone to fulfill their potential because it is finished.

Nobody needs me or you to point out their imperfections. We already know we are not perfect. When we allow the love of God to flow through us, we allow the answer to overcome the problem, and we empower people to fulfill their potential in Christ Jesus (Romans 2:4). That's why we can do all things through Christ (Philippians 4:13), because God is love, and love conquers all (1 John 4:8).

If you look at the optimism in the Word of God, it's all about you can, you will, and so forth. In Jesus, there is only potential for greatness. So as you start your day and prepare to take the good news to a lost and dying world, always remember that Jesus never acknowledged peo- ple's problems but rather their potential in Him. Let your light shine and allow God's love to change the world through you! Have a great day! Kim and I love you.

Peace Empowers

When we lose our peace, we lose our power! What is so important about peace? Peace gives us understanding according to the Word of God; it creates an atmosphere of clarity (Philippians 4:7). When we are angry, bitter, have unforgiveness, resentment, guilt, fear, loneliness, and everything this world offers, it clouds our ability to make decisions that are beneficial for our lives.

So think of this, if I am angry and have unforgiveness, then I am likely to think revenge and destruction. When we put anger down and walk in forgiveness, it empowers us to walk in love. This gives us the ability to pray for those who despitefully use us. Forgiveness isn't for the other person, it's for us (Luke 6:28). Forgiveness enables God to work in our behalf. Peace is the foundation for every good thing. Every victory we can experience in our lives is the very essence of who Jesus is! The Bible states that Jesus is the prince of peace, and only through Him can we have and do all things. The Bible states blessed is the peacemaker! Why? Because peace is the foundation for all things!

Kim and I love you have a super awesome day and strive to maintain peace doing all that God has empowered you to do!

Philosophy

Philosophy is the study of ideas about knowledge and truth about nature and the meaning of life. So what are ideas? Ways of thinking! The Bible states that we are the righteousness of God in Christ, and we have been set apart and made whole by the blood of Jesus and through Him, we can do all things. When we ask Jesus into our hearts, we become all that Jesus is. We literally become the righteousness of God, according to the Bible! It is our identity as a born-again believer! That's why Satan tries to steal our identity. Satan knows that as long as he can keep us ignorant of whom we are in Christ, we will never be able to fulfill our destiny and or purpose in Christ Jesus!

Philosophy is nothing more than a way of thinking! So why are there so many different ways of thought when it comes to life? Many philosophies are Satan's attempt to cause confusion regarding who we are and what we were created for. Jesus stated that He was the Way, the Truth, and the Life, and there was only one way to the Father. We can only fulfill our purpose in Christ if we remain in Christ. Satan doesn't care what we believe or what philosophy we study as long as it isn't *the* way, *the* truth, and the life! In the garden, Eve was created in the image of God; she was righteous. God denied Eve nothing. What did Satan do first? Satan tried to bring confusion to Eve about who she was created to be. Satan simply implied that God's word wasn't really true. Satan asked the question, (Genesis 3:3), did God say? Satan wanted to cause doubt in eve's mind, of God's faithfulness and Eve's right standing with God.

When Jesus was in the desert, what did Satan attack when he was tempting Jesus? Satan said if you are the son of God! Why? Because if he could get Jesus to lose focus on who He was and the validity of God's Word, Jesus would never of accomplished all that. He was sent to accomplish on the cross. We would still be lost and dying in our sin! The Bible states that as a man thinks, so is he (Proverbs 23:7)!

It's so vital that we understand who we are in Christ Jesus. The Word of God is true, faithful, and just, and through Christ, we can accomplish anything! Knowledge of *the* truth is power; it's what equips us to do amazing things. God says to renew our mind daily by reading the *Bible* (2 Timothy 3:16). The Bible is the inspired Word of God. It instructs us on who we are, who Jesus is, and all that we can accomplish if we learn to think like Him! The Bible states that God's people perish from a lack of knowledge or a misunderstanding of who we are and all that Jesus should be in our lives. We need to read our Bibles! Seek God, resist Satan, and he hast to flee!

The moral of the story is this, if we want to walk in victory in life, and we want to accomplish all that God has for our lives, then never allow Satan to talk us out of our identity in Christ Jesus! Now that Christ's truth has set us free, we need to go and set others free! There are people in our circles of life bound by wrong thinking, frustrated by Satan's lies, and we are literally holding the key to their freedom in our hearts. His name is Jesus!

Kim and I love you and are super excited for you in your journey! Have a great day!

Pitiful or Powerful

Pitiful or powerful, the choice is ours! The Bible says count it all joy when trials and tribulations come (James 1:2-4). Say what? Okay, so let's see what God's Word says about this issue! Most of you know that last Thursday I was in a motorcycle accident and broke my left hip and left knee. Bummer, right? The Bible says that if I will draw near to God in times of trouble, then he will take what Satan meant for harm and turn it around to bring glory and honor to his holy name! So as I lay in the hospital, Kim and I started praying with other patients, allowing God's love to flow through us. Why? Because it's the love of God through us that draws all to come to know and understand his saving grace (Romans 2:4).

I had the privilege of sharing God's plan and purpose with many. Several doctors and nurses came to know their destiny for greatness, knowing that God created them for fellowship and God had purpose for their lives. Satan meant to discourage me, but not only was God honored, but I was also blessed to love those around me. My doctors and nurses were amazed at my attitude and that we have maintained joy and peace even in pain and suffering because the greater one lives in us!

God's Word is amazing. His promises are true, faithful, and just. He is faithful, he is my provider, and he is in control! If you are in a valley today and the devil is beating you up, then run to God let your light shine and allow God to work through you. Allow others to experience his unfailing faithfulness. Walk in the power as an overcomer and refuse to be defined by adversity. Don't settle for pitiful when you have the potential to be powerful. Kim and I love you and no matter what, God is in control!

Preventive Maintenance

Why do we need preventive maintenance? When we change the oil in our car, it's to prevent engine troubles. When we rotate our tires, it's to prevent uneven wear and tear. When we change the furnace filter, it's so our furnace will operate at its peak performance, keeping us from burning up the blower motor. There are so many things in our lives that require preventive maintenance. We should never argue the need for maintenance; we should just do it. Why? Because we know that if we don't, it will reap unwanted situations in our lives. No one wants to replace a three-thousand-dollar engine in our car because we chose not to change the oil.

Just like the natural things in our lives need maintenance, so do our spiritual lives. If we don't talk to God, we will never experience a good relationship with God. If we don't read our Bibles, we will never fulfill our purpose, because what we don't know will keep us from God's best. If we don't walk in love, we can't reap love. The list goes on and on. So if we don't want the negative, then we need to do something positive.

God has an amazing plan and purpose for our lives (Jeremiah 29:11). The bottom line is we all need to have preventive maintenance in our lives. We need to pray, read our Bibles, and allow our lives to reflect all that God's Word says we can be, through his unlimited grace and his amazing faithfulness. His promises are "yes" and "amen" (2 Corinthians 1:20), and the Bible is faithful true and just. The highlight of God's day is knowing we desire to spend time with him. Kim and I love you. Have a great day!

Railroad

I recently took a job working with railroads, and I'm amazed at the way trains work. Up to this point, I never took the time to notice trains. A locomotive weighs 400,000 pounds, a full coal car weighs 200,000 pounds, and the average coal train is anywhere from 100 to 175 cars in length. Do the math, and that is one heavy load! The trains are all directed by the yardmaster, and as long as they follow instructions perfectly, they are able to reach their full potential.

In our lives, God is like the yardmaster, and as long as we follow instructions, we are able to accomplish what we were created for. The tracks are the Word of God, and as long as we remain on the tracks, we can continue to accomplish our purpose. I have seen trains derail because they weren't following instructions from the yardmaster. It takes a lot of time and effort to get the train back on the tracks. Sin tries to derail us and keep us from fulfilling our purpose! Even if we derail, it's not the end of the world. It just requires a lot more effort to get going again.

If an engineer says, "I'm going to drive this train, but I don't think I need tracks," we would say, "Are you stupid?" Even if we didn't know anything about a train, we still know that without tracks, we aren't going anywhere. Another aspect to tracks is they were laid prior to the train using them. The Word was made available for us to go forward because Jesus went before and paid the price so that his Word would carry us to our full potential! Sometimes we misuse the Word of God. We take it out of context, we wrongly apply it, and we misrepresent it, causing others to derail, resulting in mass casualties. When we listen to God and we read and apply his Word, it will take us anywhere while expanding our horizons. We are literally empowered for greatness. A locomotive can pull 12 million pounds. We are that locomotive, and the cars we are pulling are souls. As long as we follow instructions from God and we stay on track with the Word, we will accomplish all that God has for our lives. Remember, a loco- motive was not just created to pull itself; it was designed to pull many cars behind it. Just like that locomotive, we were not created to just go to heaven but to lead many to their destination in Christ. Just like a train without a locomotive won't go anywhere, there are people that won't ever reach their destination without us doing our part! Let's seek God read and apply his Word and fulfill our purpose so that others can come to know and understand their purpose in Christ Jesus! Kim and I love you and are cheering you on. Have a great day

Wrong Relationships

Have you ever been in a relationship and you could tell that the other person didn't really love you? Why do we go through the motions not out of love, but out of obligation? Have you ever expressed a need to your spouse or significant other, and they clearly only responded because you asked and not because they really wanted to? In your heart, there was no blessing attached, and in fact, you would rather they did nothing other than just go through the motions? That's often how it is with God.

His Word gives us instructions on what is pleasing and close to the heart of God, such as feeding the hungry, visiting those in prison, healing the sick, casting out devils, and so on. Jesus talked about the Day of Judgment. Jesus stated some would say we did all these things in your name, but he makes an incredible statement: "Depart from me I never knew you" (Matthew 7:22). Wow! Why is that? For the same reason, you find no joy in what your spouse does out of just obligation. It wasn't done in love!

The Bible says works without faith is dead (James 2:14-26). You can only walk in faith when fueled by love! We read our Bibles because we want to know the heart of God. We love people because it's an act of worship and it brings joy to the heart of God. This is the difference between works and worship! I encourage you to examine your heart and ask yourself why do you do what you do. No one wants to labor in vain. I don't know about you, but I don't want to waste my life doing things out of obligation only to find out it was all for nothing! Learn to love God through acts of worship knowing that your worship is a blessing to the creator of all things. Wow! There is nothing better than a relationship based on love! Kim and I love you and want great things for your lives! Have a blessed day.

Relationships

The awesomeness of a great relationship! The statistics of failed relationships are staggering! Why is it that relationships are failing in record amounts? The Bible says that in and of ourselves, we can do nothing (John 5:30). Why? Because God is love, and true love can only come from him alone (1 John 4:8). The sad part about failed relationships is it's everywhere, churches included! Why? Because people are not reading and applying God's Word! The proof is in the pudding!

It doesn't matter how good of a person you are. In your own strength, failure is imminent! Take two people arguing. They both want to be right, and usually they feel the other person in the wrong. This is a perfect example because the Bible states that true love finds no fault! Love keeps no record of wrong (1 Corinthian 13:5). This kind of love can only be found in the Word of God as you cultivate a relationship with Jesus. The Word of God instructs us on how to live a life that produces prosperous relationshiPsalms I know this because the Bible states that God prospers everything I put my hands to do (Deuteronomy 30:9). As I have applied his Word in my own life, my relationship with Kim has prospered immensely. Everywhere Kim and I go, people say they can see our love for each other, and my social media family has commented many times of our deep love for each other. The only explanation is that Kim and I read and apply God's Word and are willing to do it his way; therefore, our relationship prospers.

Many times in life two people come together and it's obvious that they are soul mates and obviously God has brought both people together. Compatibility in and of itself is not enough. They have to put God first if they are truly going to experience the blessings of a divine relationship! The beauty of putting Jesus first in our lives is that every aspect of our lives is affected by his amazing promises. When you and your spouse seek God and set the example for your children by reading your Bibles as a family and teaching them the importance of that relationship with their creator, God promises that when your children grow old, they won't depart from truth (Proverbs 22:6). Your jobs will prosper because you honor God with your money! Your life becomes whole and blessed above and beyond the more you seek God. So read your Bible, be willing to do whatever God is teaching you in his Word, and when it's all God, it will be all good! Kim and I love you and are cheering for you. Have a great day.

Faithfulness

Sometimes we allow circumstances to rob us of our faithfulness! Faithfulness to serve and seek God in our lives is a decision based on necessity. In and of ourselves, we can do nothing (2 Corinthians 3:5). Life without God is hopeless, hard, and always in crisis.

Sometimes we as people are faced with adversity in our lives. We allow the plans and schemes of our enemy to keep us from seeking God, when in reality that's when we should be the closest to God. Don't think that there will ever be a good time to serve God. Satan will always make sure there is something or someone who will deter us from seeking God. Don't rely on prayer lines and prayer teams to be your connection to God. Prayer lines can only take us so far.

When it comes down to it, the proof is in the pudding. What are we doing with what God gave us? We need to read our Bibles daily, allowing our minds to be renewed while our faith is cultivated and all while learning to fight the good fight! Why be pitiful when we have the potential to be powerful. Remember it's through Christ that we can accomplish anything! Kim and I love you. Have a great day!

Ring-Around-the-Rosy

Around and round and round we go. Where we stop, nobody knows! Sometimes we feel like our lives are going in circles. We aren't sure how to get out of the circle and on a path that allows us to fulfill our destiny?

We first need to realize our need for a Savior. Jesus is the beginning that establishes our destiny while revealing God's purpose for our lives. Wrong thinking leads to wrongdoing. Wrongdoing leads to a wrong direction. Wrong direction leaves us unhappy while searching for peace in our lives.

When we choose to lead our lives according to the Word of God, it allows us to experience the fullness of God's promises or his blessings. Our focus can never be about our problems but rather the solutions that are presented in God's Word. The truth comes from God's Word and allows everyone to walk in the freedom that it provides.

If you've gotten off track, don't sweat it. God's not disappointed or mad at us; he is mad about us. We should be quick to run to God while confessing our sins. As we seek first the kingdom in all that we do, say, and think, then everything else will be freely given to us (Matthew 6:33).

So if you find yourself going in a circle, stop! Think about the last issue that God was working on with you. Was it impatience, unforgiveness, ungratefulness, bad attitude, whatever it might be, repent! We can only be effective in walking forward when the past is firmly placed behind us. God loves us and will do amazing things in us, through us, and for us if we allow him to lead us. Kim and I are cheering for you. Have a great day.

No Condemnation in Christ

A friend of mine once made the comment that they felt condemned and guilty after attending church. Many times the message has been misrepresented. People often point the finger while judging people's sin rather than helping them see their potential in Christ. Jesus made a profound statement, "I didn't come to condemn the world but to save it" (John 3:17). Jesus is the light of the world (John 8:12). Light is an amazing thing, and when applied to our lives, it reveals the dark corners of our hearts. The light helps us to remove the hindrances while helping us reach our full potential in experiencing God's plan and purpose for our lives.

The Bible states that out of the heart flow the issues of life (Proverbs 4:23). The beauty of the Word of God is it teaches us how to think. The Word gives us a productive life that reflects the abundance of life that Jesus so freely gives us. The Bible states as a man thinks in his heart, so is he (Proverbs 23:7). So as the light of Jesus is hidden in our heart through reading and applying the Word of God to our lives, it reveals the darkness or the wrong ways of thinking. This darkness or wrong thinking actually keeps us from God's very best when fulfilling our purpose in this earth. Darkness renders us ineffective when shining the light on those around us.

When someone doesn't know or hasn't experienced Jesus, they are imprisoned in life's darkness because they don't know how to think other than what the world offers. When we begin to lead an abundant life full of love, mercy, grace, and compassion, it allows the light or Jesus to overflow into the lives around us. This brings hope to the hopeless, healing to the brokenhearted, and a love that can conquer anything Jesus didn't come to condemn. If we are a true reflection of who and what he truly is, then we too should never condemn or judge someone because of the sin or type of sin that is causing them to stumble. We should walk in love, allowing the faithfulness of God's mercy, grace, and compassion to transform their lives restoring them to the fullness of all that God has in store for them. Always remember, just because the message is misrepresented doesn't mean the message is wrong; it just means the person presenting the message is wrong. Kim and I love you. Have a super awesome day, and know that we are cheering for you.

The Power of Prayer

We have had many race issues throughout the years. We have had no shortage of demonstrations or rioting. I am all for equality. I don't believe that any man should be considered more or less of a person in the eyes of others. Opportunities that are given to a person should not be due to color, race, or creed. With that said, I would like to look at racism according to the Word of God!

Race is not an issue of color! I know that this statement strikes a chord in the hearts of many, but let's take a deeper look at the issue. Satan has made this issue personal, and it's not personal! We wrestle not against flesh or blood but against principalities and the powers of darkness (Ephesians 6:12). Our fight is spiritual. The last 250 years, we have been fighting a spiritual battle in a natural manner! If we would have spent half as much time on our knees seeking God as we have been on our feet demonstrating, we would not have a race issue at all. The devil distracts and distorts the truth because he knows that it's the truth that sets us free (John 8:32). What exactly is the truth?

Well, for one, the Bible states that God is not a respecter of persons (Acts 10:34, Romans 2:11). Neither should we be! God states that we have authority over all the plans and schemes of the enemy (Luke 10:19). Racism isn't a problem that can't be fixed; it's just we are going about it all wrong! The Bible states that when we pray according to the Word of God, God not only hears our prayers but that he will answer them (1 John 5:14). Maybe our prayers are misdirected, or we are not praying at all.

The Word of God empowers our prayers. God states that he watches over his Word to perform it, and when we utilize God's Word, it will not return void (Isaiah 55:11). The Bible also states that it's the love of God through us that draws all men to a place of understanding of what Jesus accomplished on the cross (Romans 2:4). This is for our salvation and the fullness of his love.

The Simplicity of a Practical Jesus

Our nation has turned its back on God. We have kicked God out of our schools, courts, military, and nation. Our television and radio programming is anything but a reflection of God's love. We the people as a whole are self-absorbed with an entitlement mentality! The core of our problem is a sin issue, not a race issue. If we would turn from our wickedness, God would hear our prayers and heal this land.

The power of God's Word is amazing, and God's love can conquer all. Wanting the benefits of God's love and applying God's love are two totally different things. We talk that we want to live in peace and harmony, where it's all good all the time, but it takes more than just wanting it. We need to seek God first in all we do, say, and think. God's love will bring freedom and healing. God's love ushers his blessings not only on a personal level but on a national level as well. If we are not careful, the day will come when God will withdraw, and we will be left with what we have sown. The Bible states let a man not be fooled in his heart, for whatever he sows, he will reap (Galatians 6:7). Without God's love, darkness will destroy life as we know it. The good news is that his mercies are new every morning, and God is a god of restoration (Lamentations 3:22-23). The Bible says as a man thinks, so is he (Proverbs 23:7). If our nation is a reflection of darkness, then maybe we as a nation are thinking wrongly. Just saying!

God's mercies endure forever (Psalms 136:1). We aren't waiting for his promises, because his promises are "yes" and "amen" (2 Corinthians 1:20). God is waiting for us to walk in the fullness of his Word (Ephesians 3:19). Our obedience to God's truth sets the captives free and will heal our land. The Word of God states that one person equipped with God's Word can put a thousand to flight (Joshua 23:10, Deuteronomy 22:30, Leviticus 26:8). Two people united in God's Word are empowered to put ten thousand to flight. If we would unite as a nation, empowered with God's Word, we would literally be the most powerful nation in the world. Kim and I love you and are thankful for God's amazing plan and purpose for your life! Have a great day.

Building Our House on the Rock versus Sand

The Word of God states that Jesus was the stone the builders rejected (Psalms 118:22). Jesus is the rock. Jesus talked about building our lives on the rock, and when the storms of life come, they won't move us (Matthew 7:24-27). When we build our lives on the sands of life, it only takes one good storm to destroy us. We have a certain level of peace that comes from knowing that the storms of life can't move us because of the foundation provided for us.

Jesus was the Word made flesh (John 1:14). Everything in the Bible represents who Jesus is in written form. The Bible instructs us to read our Bibles daily. When we know God, we can think like God. When we think right, our lives automatically go in the right direction. Our footsteps are divinely ordered (Psalms 37:23). The Word of God is a lamp unto our feet, giving us the ability to see where we are headed (Psalms 119:105).

The Bible not only helps us to know Christ better but it gives us the ability to overcome every plan and scheme that Satan would try and use against us. The Word teaches us how to think, speak, live, and have our being. I don't know about you, but I don't want to just go to heaven. I want all that is available to me through God's Word! You can be powerful or pitiful. The difference between the two is reading and applying the Word of God. Kim and I love you, and know that God has an amazing plan and purpose for your lives! Have a great day.

Salvation Is Just the Beginning

Have you ever known someone who has asked Jesus in their life but that's as far as it went? It seems as if they always have a bad attitude, and if they had one positive thought, their brain just might lock up! Having Jesus in our hearts and knowing Jesus personally are opposite ends of the spectrum.

The Bible says when we walk in the spirit, we will not fulfill the lust of our human nature (Galatians 5:16). How do we walk in the spirit? By reading and applying the Word of God in our lives daily! If we want to accomplish greatness, walk in victory and experience all that God has for us, then we have to be a student of his Word! Have you ever tried to put something together without reading the instructions? After all, how hard can it be? Three hours later you just want to throw the project in the trash! Instructions are for the purpose of making things easier.

Everything that God has for our lives—his plans, purpose, will, desires, and promises and every good thing that comes from reading and applying his Word—have been made available to us because of what Jesus accomplished on the cross! We need to rise and shine, seek God in his Word every morning, pray, and ask him to reveal himself to us through his Word. We should always walk in God's love, allowing others to see Jesus in us! Kim and I love you and are excited for all that God has in store for you! Have a super awesome day.

Satan Is Our Accuser

Satan comes to steal kill and destroy (John 10:10-29). The Bible never states that we won't have to face trials in our lives. Nor does the Bible state that we will never have to fight the enemy. In fact, God gives us armor (Ephesians 6:10-18), he instructs us on how to put the armor on, and he comforts us in stating that no weapon formed against us will prosper (Isaiah 54:17). We are empowered with all authority over principalities and powers of darkness.

When Joseph was working for Potifer and Potifer's wife wrongly accused Joseph of rape, Joseph stayed focused, and God worked it out to Joseph's favor (Genesis 39). When Daniel was thrown in the lions' den, he rested in knowing that God was in control, and he was able to lie down and sleep while surrounded by lions (Daniel 43). When Shadrach, Meshach, and Abednego were thrown in the fiery furnace, they rejoiced knowing God was in control (Daniel 3:23). Always remember Satan would not take the time and effort to come against us if we were not a threat. That's why the Bible states we should count it all joy in trails and tribulations (James 1:2).

First of all, God has our back, and second, Satan is scared. We can't waste time trying to defend our integrity or our character. When we are a reflection of Jesus, then it's not about our character; it's about his character! The battle is not personal—it's spiritual (Ephesians 6:12). This is a battle only God can win! No matter how bleak the battle looks, no matter how many witnesses the enemy rallies, the promises of God are "yes" and "amen" (2 Corinthians 1:20). What Satan means for our harm, God will turn it around for his glory. We need to stay focused, continue to do what we know is right in the eyes of God, and be faithful to Jesus. The Bible says when we have done all we can do, stand (Ephesians 6:13). The truth will set us free (John 8:32). God has called all of us to accomplish greatness. Don't be fooled! Greatness can't be achieved without opposition! Kim and I love you and are excited to see what God is doing in you, through you, and for you. Keep Jesus first! Have a great day.

Satan Knows the Word of God

Satan uses God's Word to discourage us. Have you ever fought with someone, and they were totally predictable? Well, the good news is Satan is not only the father of lies but he is also using the same lies today that he used six thousand years ago in the Garden of Eden (John 8:44). God had given Eve everything that was good for her to enjoy. God also created Eve in his image (Genesis 1:27). Satan told Eve that she couldn't eat the apple because God didn't want her to be like him. Eve was already like God. Satan asked, "Has God said?" (Genesis 3:1).

I was driving down the interstate on my motorcycle and was feeling overwhelmed, defeated, and on the verge of being depressed. I am always amazed at how fast our feelings jump on the band wagon reinforcing our thoughts. The Bible states that we should take our thoughts captive to the pulling down of strongholds (2 Corinthians 10:5). What exactly does this mean?

When we don't stop the negative and start speaking God's promises, Satan literally builds a stronghold in our minds. This gives Satan access and takes us to a dark place in our minds. The other thing Satan is good at is using the Word of God against us. While I was riding along, I heard Satan say God's Word states God will provide our needs (Philippians 4:19). Satan continued, "Look at your situation. God isn't providing for you. The Bible is just an old storybook. Quit wasting your time believing in something you can't have!" All of a sudden, I realized Satan is the father of lies, and he knows no truth (John 8:44). I began to speak the promises of God over my life while cruising down the highway. All of a sudden I could feel hope and peace rise up inside me. I got excited and started speaking with the authority that God gives us to claim his amazing promises.

Do you know what happened? Within minutes, I had my joy back and certainty in my heart that God's promises were true, and the darkness that was fighting for my mind was gone. The joy of the Lord became my strength (Psalms 28:7). Wow!

Satan knows that if he can get us thinking wrongly, our lives will literally go in the wrong direction. Where the mind goes, the man follows. That's what I'm talking about. God is awesome, and his Word is true. He is faithful, true, and just (Psalms 33:4). His promises are "yes" and "amen", and the devil is a liar! Don't let the enemy rip you off. Learn the Word of God so that you too can speak to the mountains in your life and watch God's faithfulness work in your behalf! Kim and I love you and are excited to see God working in your lives. Have a great afternoon!

Satan's Failure/God's Victory

I was reading in the book of Esther this morning, and as usual, I was amazed not only at God's timing but his faithfulness as well. The Bible states that God knows the end from the beginning (Isaiah 46:10). In reality, God has an answer before there is a problem. How amazing is that?

In the book of Esther, the queen at that time became comfortable in her success, and pride kept her from doing what was right. Because of the queen's pride, she lost everything she had. Not only did Satan rob her of her blessing, but God removed her from office. God filled the position with someone who was faithful, despite her lack of qualifications for the job. Esther's heart was pure, and she honored God with her life, and because of this, she was elevated to the position of queen, and she had favor beyond compare.

When we live our lives based on the Word of God and we honor God with our thoughts, words, and deeds, he works in our behalf and our lives are a reflection of his faithfulness.

The other part of this story is equally amazing. There was a guy named Haymon, and he too was prideful and vindictive. Instead of using his place of authority to help others and be a blessing to those around him, he had a prideful heart and was all about himself. If this wasn't bad enough, he despised a righteousness man named Mordecai and went as far as to plot his death. The Bible states that no weapon formed against us will prosper and every tongue that rises against us in judgment will be proved to be in the wrong (Isaiah 54:17). This story is a perfect example of God's faithfulness. Mordecai didn't even know that Haymon was plotting his death, and before he even found out, God turned the situation around for his glory and Mordecai benefit. God gave Mordecai favor with the king, and Haymon was ordered to parade Mordecai around dressed in fine robes while leading him on a donkey and proclaiming what a faithful servant Mordecai was. This was a two-fold deal. First, this was a life lesson for Haymon in humility, to repent of his prideful heart. Second,

Mordecai was being honored for his faithfulness in serving God. Haymon did not turn from his wicked, prideful heart and plotted to hang Mordecai. The Bible says that when our enemies dig a hole for our destruction, they themselves fall in it (Psalms 7:15, Proverbs 26:27). Haymon had a gallows made to hang Mordecai, and what he intended for Mordecai's defeat ended in Haymon's demise.

This story has a third part. Haymon plotted the death of all the Jews. Before this was ever a thought in Haymon's twisted little mind, God had a plan to place Esther as queen to protect his people. Haymon's plan played out, but because Esther's faith and trust were in the Lord, she sought God's face through fasting and praying, and God delivered his people.

Sometimes we have to endure Satan's plan, but if we put our faith and trust in God, we will always overcome while displaying God's faithfulness in our lives for others to see. The test always becomes the testimony. The Bible states that no matter what Satan intends for our harm, if we will trust our Creator, it will turn out for God's glory and our benefit. This is a perfect win-win situation. Kim and I love you and are excited to watch you walk in the provision of God's faithfulness. Have a great day.

Simple

According to the *Webster* dictionary, the meaning of *simple* is "not hard to understand or do; not complex or fancy."

Jesus stated that we should have a childlike faith (Matthew 18:3). Christianity has been so twisted and blown out of proportion. Sometimes we represent something other than what the gospel really is. We often tell others of God's provision, but we don't walk in God's provision ourselves. We tend to have all the right words but no fruit that bears witness of God's faithfulness. We have so many different denominations because we can't even agree on the basic foundations of what we are supposed to believe.

The Bible states that a house that is divided can't stand (Mark 3:25). Satan understands the power of division and is good at playing the game. Jesus was always bringing people together everywhere he traveled. His love for the people was felt by all. When was the last time the love of God through us actually made a difference in someone else's life?

I know a lady that went to a job interview, and the girl interviewing her stopped and asked, "Are you always this happy? There is just something about you." The lady answered, "I have Jesus living in my heart." She didn't have to say anything; the love of God was freely flowing from her life. Jesus also had the love of God flowing through him. He often stated, "If you have seen me, you have seen the father. The father and I are one" (John 14:9). As Jesus allowed his father's love to freely flow, we too should be able to say, "If you have seen me, you have seen Jesus!"

We need to live our lives as a reflection of Jesus and literally draw all men to understand God's plan and purpose for their lives. Simple, not hard to understand or do. Not complex or fancy! Kim and I love you and are excited for others to experience Jesus through you. Have a great day.

Sin

S̲ecret I̲nfectious N̲egativity! Sin is nothing more than Satan's plan to keep us from God's best. Satan often dresses sin up with glitz and glamour while using our emotions to build excitement and anticipation. Satan often uses television and other sorts of programming to propagate or justify what we know is really wrong, is really okay. Satan's greatest schemes also include secrets. Secrets are dangerous because when we have a secret, there is always the potential that someone will come to know our secret. Our secrets can be used as leverage to exposes the very thing we know in our heart is wrong. The reason that secrets are so infectious is because sin has an appetite that always has a need to be fed. One small sin has the potential to grow into something so big it could bring utter destruction in our lives. When planting an acorn, we see a small insignificant seed, but the potential for a massive oak tree is inevitable. Sin doesn't just infect our lives with this destructive negativity but it also hurts and infects those around us. Satan's hope is that he can infect us to the point of death while claiming our souls for eternity.

The Bible states that our thoughts become words, which become sin, and when full-grown, they produce death or separation from God's plan and purpose for our lives (James 1:15). Satan's next agenda after talking us into willful disobedience is to write in the eyes of God guilt and condemnation. Guilt and condemnation are tools that, at best, keep us in a place that breeds hopelessness, loneliness, and sure destruction in our lives. The Bible states that Satan is our accuser (1 Timothy 4:13). The same person that sells us on the idea of sin is the same that accuses and condemns us. This is the slippery slope of destruction. Satan comes to steal, kill, and destroy (John 10:10-29). He wants to steal our potential in Christ, kill our dreams, and destroy any opportunity of relationship with our creator. The good news is this, when we walk in a dark room and flip on a light, the darkness leaves, and the light exposes what was once hidden.

The Simplicity of a Practical Jesus

The Bible teaches us to confess our sins (1 John 1:9). Why? Because God knows that when we do we are no longer bound by that secret and Satan is powerless in keeping us from the saving grace of Jesus. The Bible states that a righteous man falls seven times but gets back up (Proverbs 24:16-18). When we are quick to confess our sins, God is faithful to forgive us our sins. God's love conquers all (1 Corinthians 13). As we read and apply God's Word to our lives, we are empowered to do the impossible. Let go and let God because, when it's all God, it's all good. Kim and I love you. Have a great day.

Know Your Enemy

The greatest way to win a war is to know your enemy! When you know who you're fighting and the way they think, their limitations, and their abilities, then and only then can you successfully overcome victoriously! So how does Satan over come and defeat us? Satan knows what we don't, he sees what we don't see, and he knows the Word of God better than us. This is Satan's strongest weapon against us!

The Bible states that we have all authority over all principalities and powers of darkness (Ephesians 1:21), yet Satan is winning! Why? Because he knows what we should but don't! The Bible instructs us to be as wise as a serpent and as gentle as a dove (Matthew 10:16). The Bible states that if we are lacking wisdom, ask and it will be given to us (James 1:5). We also need to study the Word of God so that when we are at war, we can operate in victory rather than defeat! We have all wisdom available to us; all we have to do is ask.

So why should we be as gentle as a dove? Because peace passes understanding (Philippians 4:7) and the definition of *gentle* according to the *Webster* dictionary is "having or showing a kind and gentle nature, not harsh or violent nor hard or forceful." See, when we truly understand the love of God, who we are in Christ Jesus, and the power that we posses over all principalities, then it's as simple as walking in the truth that comes from knowing God's Word. If the truth effortlessly sets the captives free and that same truth lives in us, then we don't have to rant and rave, and we don't need to judge or be obnoxious. We just need to allow the gentleness of Jesus and his love permeate our lives. God's love conquers all!

Satan takes our Christianity and uses it to misrepresent the love of God, therefore discrediting our mission and God's faithfulness Instead of allowing God's love through us to draw all to the understanding of who God is, it keeps people from experiencing truth. When there is no truth, people will never understand the freedom from Satan's bondage! We should be winning, but instead we are losing!

Sin is sin, and no matter how dark this world becomes, the Bible states that God's grace is always greater. Learn God's Word, and equip yourselves to walk in victory and be empowered to set the cap- tives free. God has an amazing plan and purpose for our lives, and the only thing that determines our success or failure is our willingness to gain truth (Jeremiah 29:11). Allow God's love to drive you! Anything else is failure! Kim and I love you. Have a great day!

Start a Fire in My Soul, Lord. Fan the Flames and Make It Grow

What is our soul? Our soul is our mind, will, and emotions. The soul is who we are before we experience Jesus. Prior to Jesus, we think and feel according to circumstances or the world's way of thinking. When we ask Jesus into our lives, our spirit is given birth, and we are now able to see things as God sees them. As we begin to read and apply God's Word to our lives, our soul begins to prosper and conform to God's plan and purpose for our lives.

Many times people ask Jesus into their lives, giving life to the spirit, but never seek truth through God's Word; therefore, they never experience God's full plan and purpose for their lives. You can't think and feel things that are contrary to truth and expect truth to change your life. This is what is referred to as hope deferred, and it leaves us sick in our heart (Proverbs 13:12). We can only live right when we think right. The Bible states that as a man thinks in his heart, so is he (Proverbs 23:7), and out of the heart flow the issues of life (Proverbs 4:23). If you don't like the direction your life is going, then change the way you think. The Bible instructs us to renew our minds daily by reading and applying God's truths to our lives (Ephesians 4:23, Romans 12:2). The fire that has started in our soul is the beginning of our relationship with God.

As we seek him out in his Word, we literally fan the flames. God's fire consumes the things in our lives that are contrary to truth while refining the things that are of worth (Matthew 7:19). The refining fire takes what is valuable with an ordinary look, and it makes it into what it was designed to be, revealing the fullness of God's glory (Malachi 3:3). The Bible states that everything in our lives either now or the life to come will go through the fire of God's Word. The things that are worthless and of wrong motive will burn up, but the things that we cultivate in our lives that are founded on truth will reflect God's goodness and his perfect love in us and through us (1 Corinthians 3:15). When we embrace the fire of God, asking him to make it grow, we will not only see his perfect will for our lives but also experience a sweet relationship with our creator. God desires relationship with each and every one of us (1 Corinthians 1:9, Genesis 3:8, Revelation 4:11). We all have potential for greatness, and in Christ, we can do all things (Philippians 4:13). Kim and I love you and want the very best for you. We are excited to see the beauty of God revealed in your life as you allow the Word of God to make you all that God is and wants for you. Have a great day.

Superheroes

Have you ever stopped and considered how superheroes became superheroes? We all love a good superhero. They are selfless, wholesome, and have everyone else's interest at heart.

Superman came from a planet far away. His parents were killed by the destruction of his planet, and he was sent to live on earth, where he could never again see his family. In school growing up, he always knew he was different, and because he couldn't disclose his differences, he lived his life lonely with no close friends. Despite all that Superman faced in life, it didn't keep him from fulfilling his purpose in this earth. Batman came from a wealthy family that could afford anything. Yet his mom and dad were murdered, and he was left to be raised by bats, and he too was not able to share his deepest, darkest secrets. However, he still fulfilled his purpose in the earth. Spiderman was left to live with his aunt and uncle and was bitten by a spider. Peter's uncle was murdered, leaving Peter Parker to cope with this great loss. The Hulk was a loner who was in an industrial accident and forced to live a life on the run. David Banner never really had the opportunity to experience a close relationship.

We often file into the theaters with many others that seek the next adventure or accomplishment of the superhero as they overcome the bad guy. The bad guy or the villain also has experienced horrible situations, but they take the tragedy, and they allow it to make them bitter, selfish, and destructive in nature. The Joker fell in a vat of acid and was disfigured. And he became Batman's nemesis. The Penguin was abandoned by his parents because of the abnormality of his birth defects and turned to the dark side

The whole point is, we all have a sad story to tell. We all have the choice of allowing God to bring healing in our lives and helping us to fulfill our purpose in this earth. We can also choose to allow our circumstance to define us and rob us of any potential that allows us to see greatness in our lives. Will you allow your adversity to bring hope to someone else's life, or will you allow your adversity to destroy someone else's life?

The Bible states that all things good or bad work together for good to those who love God and are called according to his purpose (Romans 8:28). The good news is, it's not God's desire that any man perish (2 Peter 3:9), and all are called according to his purpose. The difference is, some choose life and others except death. Choose this day whom you will serve (Joshua 24:15). Kim and I love you and are excited to see God exchange your misfortune for his fortune, helping you to overcome what Satan meant for harm while reaching your full potential in Christ. Have a great day.

Tasty Fruit

What does your fruit taste like? The Bible says that we will be known by the fruit we bear (Matthew 7:16). What is good fruit, and how do we obtain it in our lives? The Bible says that faith plus works equals good fruit! The Word also states that works without faith is dead or fruitless (James 2:14-26). Where does faith come from?

Faith comes from reading and applying the Word of God (Romans 10:17). The Bible states that whatever a man sows, that will he reap (Galatians 6:7). The more we allow God's Word to get inside us and the more we apply it the greater, the faith we will have. Works are the application of our faith in the Word of God as we apply it in our lives. God's Word empowers us to have a good attitude even though we have an opportunity to be a negative Nancy. We are empowered to meet someone's need out of love even when we could easily turn our eyes and pretend we don't see the need. Works are a result of God's love through us. The Bible states that God's love (Romans 2:4) through us literally draws all to a place of repentance or understanding of who Jesus is and what he did for them.

The flip side of this is rotten fruit. Are we displaying a bad attitude? Do we cut people down with our words rather than build them up? Do we seem to always be a downer instead of having a positive attitude? Nobody likes rotten fruit! But good fruit is appealing to the eyes, its smell causes the mouth to water, and it's sweet and gives life or nutrients to those around us. A life built on the Word of God causes great faith. Great faith inspires great works or acts of worship that produces nice, juicy, life-giving fruit.

Allow your life to bring nutrients to the people around you. The Bible states God seeks to find a faithful heart that he can bless or use (2 Chronicles 16:9). Kim and I love you and know that God has great things for your life. Have a great day!

The Greater the Opposition, the Greater the Purpose

Kim and I recently started working with the developmentally disabled. The people we work with range from mildly retarded to totally profound. We work with autistic and Down syndrome as well. This has been our vision for several years. When the opportunity to work with these individuals was presented, we just knew it was an answer to prayers.

This week has been full of opposition from every side. Kim and I have been doing nineteen-hour days for weeks and have been very diligent to honor God with what we are doing. Opposition is really opportunity in disguise. I found myself allowing the enemy to use this opposition to become personal. My feelings were hurt, and I found myself faced with choices. Do I walk in truth and extend God's love, or do I allow offense to keep me from reaching and experiencing the fullness of God's plan for my life (Proverbs 19:11, Proverbs 18:19)? I often write these inspirationals in hopes that they not only encourage others to walk in truth, but that these same principles apply to my life as well. I left work feeling defeated, but I took my thoughts captive (2 Corinthians 10:4), began to speak God's Word over the problem, and put some praise and worship music on. The Bible states that when we take our thoughts captive and align them with the Word of God, several things happen. We literally draw close to God, and Satan hastes to flee (James 4:7).

The Bible also states that when we speak God's Word over the problem, God himself watches over his Word to perform it (Jeremiah 1:12), and his Word will accomplish what it was sent to do (Isaiah 55:11). The last thing is this, darkness always disappears when the light is turned on (John 1:5), and God inhabits the praises of his people (Psalms 22:3). When we choose to focus in the midst of adversity and keep our faith and trust in who God is and all that he is doing, then our opposition is literally transformed into the potential for God's greatness. The Bible states that whatever Satan means for harm, God

115

will use to bring glory to his holy name and work it out for our benefit (Genesis 50:20). This is called a win-win situation. When it's all God, its all good! The enemy is defeated and peace is restored.

So as I sit here writing, I'm taking what Satan meant to discourage me with, and I'm using it to encourage you as well as myself. God is not a man that he should lie (Numbers 23:19), and we can put our faith and trust in every word that is written in the Bible (Psalms 146:3). God's promises are "yes" and "amen" (2 Corinthians 1:20). So let's take the time as we go about our day and thank God for all that he has provided us in his Word. We serve a mighty God! Have a great day, and always remember, Kim and I love you and are cheering you on.

The Greener Grass

The grass is greener on the other side according to the Word of God. In Psalms 23, it states that we can walk by still waters and lie in green pastures. So let's evaluate both sides of the fence.

A yard that has no eye appeal due to brown spots, patchiness, ruts, and such is a result of no water or nutrients. This is just a lack of effort and an overall attitude of neglect. The grass on the other side of the fence is green, thick, soft, and appealing to anyone looking at it. The greener grass is what everyone is looking for; otherwise, people wouldn't seek the greener side of the fence. Greener grass is due to hard work, long hours of cultivating, regular doses of fertilizer, and hours of groom- ing.

Many times we seek greener grass but are not willing to do what is required to keep and maintain the greener grass. The still waters are a result of peace that is cultivated by reading and applying God's Word to our lives. God's peace allows us to trust him when things seem to be in turmoil or disrepair (Colossians 3:19). This peace is priceless. The green pastures are a result of the peace that comes from the still waters. Still water is good water; it provides nutrition to our spirit and allows us to maintain green grass or the outward appear- ance of God's faithfulness in our lives.

When we enjoy and display God's faithfulness in our lives, it creates desire in the people around us. Everyone wants the greener grass! Our lives are a reflection of God's faithfulness that literally allows other people to enjoy the fruit of God's faithfulness.

We need to realize that in order to have that luscious thick grass, there has to be fertilizer. In short, fertilizer is made from animal dung. Nobody likes to handle or smell dung, but it is what's necessary if we are to have greener grass! The peace that comes from the still waters equips us to handle the stinkiness of the dung, allowing the dung to bring forth the beauty of that greener grass. So let's read our Bibles and apply God's truths to our lives and allow his love, mercy, and compassion to cultivate the greener pastures that are intended for our rest. Kim and I love you. Have a great day.

The Holidays

Christmas is over, and the everyday hum of life is getting back to norMalachi It's always nice to have a holiday that at least, if not for a brief moment, gives humanity the opportunity to acknowledge Jesus and the purpose of his birth. We love driving through the different subdivisions looking at Christmas lights while soaking in the colorful beauty they so freely offer. The blinking, dancing glow of Christmas represents the true light of Jesus in us. Jesus the light of the world (John 8:12).

Don't turn your light off until next year, but allow Jesus to shine in you for the next 364 days. The Bible states that Jesus in us is a light in a dark and dying world (John 1:5). It's not what we say that allows people to see Jesus in us, but what we do. The Bible states that it's the love of God through us that draws all men to a place of understanding of who Jesus is and all that God has for our lives (Romans 2:4).

How exactly do we maintain peace in our own lives while allowing God's amazing love to shine? By drawing close to God (James 4:8, Psalms 100:2-4). When we take time to read our Bibles, spend time in prayer while seeking God's best for our lives we are empowered to reach the lost and dying, bringing glory and honor to the creator of all things (Haggai 2:9). Today is the beginning of the rest of our lives, and the rest of our lives will be the best of our lives! God's not mad at us; he's mad about us! Have a great day, and never forget Kim and I love you.

The Importance of a Good Foundation

What is your foundation? Sometimes in life we build our lives on experiences rather than on God's truth! For example, if someone grows up and is abused physically, mentally, emotionally, or sexually, it's easy to allow that situation to define the rest of their life. Many times we are unaware that one has to do with the other.

I knew a girl years ago that was abused sexually as a young child. This young lady allowed that situation to set the standard for every relationship from then on. She would have boyfriends that continue to be an abusive force in her life. Instead of running away from the abuse, she was seeking their approval. She thought that if she could please them while being faithful, she could help her abusers. In the long run, she would end up a broken, lonely, and confused person. She never experienced the beauty of what true love is.

I also knew a man who grew up seeking the approval of his parents. Approval was always within reach but never attainable. According to the world's standards, this man was successful. He had a good job, nice home, and a great car. The lack of approval that he desired infected every relationship he had his marriage, his relationships at work, and with his kids. His relationships became more and more distant and strained. As his need for approval gained momentum, he worked harder and longer, only to lose it all in the end. He never experienced feeling the satisfaction of true success!

Why do we base our lives on deceptions? Jesus said that when you build your house on the sand, it will never stand the test of time and will only leave you in despair (Matthew 7:24-27). When you build your house on God and allow his truths to define you, then and only then will you ever know the sweet success of his amazing love! His Word states we are the apple of his eye (Zachariah 2:8); he is the same yesterday, today, and forevermore (Hebrews 13:8); he will never leave us or forsake us (Deuteronomy 31:6), and he is the giver of life (Psalms 36:9).

The Simplicity of a Practical Jesus

No matter where you have been or what you have done, stop allowing the deceptions of life to define you. Allow God's faithfulness and his Word to transform your life into the awesomeness of his faithfulness and experience life as God intended it to be (Romans 12:2). God loves you; he has an amazing plan and purpose for you (Jeremiah 29:11). The only thing that will keep us from God's purpose is our unwillingness to let go and allow God (Jeremiah 9:25-26). Kim and I love you and pray that you fulfill your destiny in Jesus. Have a super awesome day!

The Joys of Fishing

Have you ever been fishing with someone and they wanted to fish but they didn't want to bait or remove the fish from the hook? When are we willing to go the extra distance in a situation like this? We might say this is just ridiculous. We might conclude by stating if you want the trophy, you have to get your hands dirty. When my boys were little, I myself didn't enjoy the efforts of fishing. My boys on the other hand couldn't wait to go fishing.

Sometimes we have to put our own wants and desires aside while helping others until they are able to do their own dirty work! Some might say, "I guess we aren't going since you aren't willing to bait your own hook?" Sometimes there is beauty in doing the dirty work so that someone else can experience the joy of God's many blessings (John 15:13). It's called grace!

Have you ever wanted the benefit of something and someone else helped you through the hard times? The Bible says the love of God through us draws all men to an understanding of Jesus's saving grace (Romans 12:2). God doesn't promise everything will be candy and spice and everything nice.

Sometimes God asks us to bait other people's hooks not because they can't, but, rather, because it's just sweeter to catch the big fish without doing the work! For example, I have been mentoring a friend in the things of God. I have instructed him on the principals of tithing. His outlook was based on his circumstance rather than God's promises. Money was tight, so my friend decided that he just didn't have enough to tithe. I knew that if I could get him to understand, he would go from not enough to more than enough. Last Tuesday night, he was at church, and I gave him ten dollars for seed money to give an offering. I prayed that God would reveal himself to my friend by bringing the increase that God's Word talks about when tithing. My friend gave the ten dollars, and within two days, my friend was hired to lay some flooring and made one hundred dollars for one day's work! If I wouldn't have baited my friend's hook, he wouldn't have experienced God's goodness! Because of my willingness to do the dirty work, my friend now understands the benefits of applying God's Word and the principles of tithing.

Is there someone in your life that needs you to put the worm on their hook? Sometimes there is great glory in doing someone else's dirty work. We have opportunities to show God's love to the lost and dying every day. Are you willing to lay down your life for another (John 15:13)? Have a great day. Kim and I love you.

Kirk Ratliff

The Next Level

The journey of spiritual growth! No one really likes the journey. We often are stretched in areas of our lives that were once comfortable. Uncomfortable situations are required as we apply the Word of God to our journey. We can only get to the next level when we are fully stretched, leaving our comfort zone for a new one. The journey or test doesn't make us who we are; it reveals who we are in Christ Jesus!

When gold is refined, we start with gold and end with gold. What is it about the process that makes the gold more valuable? The difference is, the furnace refines and removes all the imperfections, revealing its true worth (1 Peter 1:7, Isaiah 48:10, Proverbs 17:3, Psalms 66:10). When God is refining us, he uses the pressures of life's test to remove our imperfections and reveal the true beauty of Jesus in us. The refining process allows others to see all that God intended us to be.

The righteousness of God in Christ is set apart and made whole by all that Jesus accomplished on the cross (2 Corinthians 5:21). The key to achieving our full potential in life is embracing the journey (Romans 5:3), reading the Word daily (Romans 12:2), and applying everything that God reveals to us in his Word (James 1:22). Unrefined diamonds just look like rocks, but when refined, cut, and polished, they become desirable and extremely valuable. The same applies to us. The more we are refined, cut, and polished by the Word of God, the more our worth is revealed, making us extremely desirable and valuable.

The Word states that we become so desirable that the love of God in us literally draws all men to come to know and understand God's saving grace (Romans 2:4). So let's stay focused and know that God is doing a great work in us, for us, and through us (Philippians 1:6). When we stay the course, we are empowered to accomplish greatness. Kim and I love you. Have great day.

The Root of All Evil

Have you ever heard someone say that money is the root of all evil? This is one of the most misquoted scriptures in all of God's Word! It's the <u>love</u> of money that is the root of all evil (1 Timothy 6:10).

God wants all his people to live in abundance (Ephesians 3:20). Why? Because if we are broken, busted, and disgusted, first, no one will follow us, and second, if we can't meet our needs, how can we meet the needs of others? If you look through the Bible, all of God's people had great wealth. They understood a right relationship with money. They tithed on everything, and they honored God with the first fruits of everything! The Bible states that when we honor God with our tithes and offerings, he will open the windows of heaven and pour out a blessing we can't even contain (Proverbs 3:9, Malachi 3:10). If God can't get it through us, then he can't get it to us! God doesn't need our money; he wants our heart (Matthew 22:37). God has called us to feed the hungry, clothe the naked, and allow his love to flow through us (Isaiah 58:10-12). When we allow God's love to flow through us, we draw all to a place of understanding of who God is and all that he has for their lives (Romans 2:4).

Experience God's greatness firsthand! When we honor God with our money, he puts his super on our natural, and our lives are empowered to do great things and change lives, while bringing hope and love to a lost and dying world. Here is the skinny! We should never allow pride to take credit for what we have accomplished. We should never allow a spirit of poverty to shame us of the blessings of prosperity. We should give all glory honor and praise to God (Colossians 3:17, 1 Peter 4:10). We need to honor God with every dollar that comes our way. This allows God to stretch our dollars, empowering us to go and conquer the world. Kim and I love you and pray for you every day that God's plan and purpose be fulfilled in your lives. Enjoy the rest of your day.

The Secret Power of Speaking God's Word

The Bible states that out of the abundance of the heart, the mouth speaks (Luke 6:45). God's Word also states that the powers of life and death, blessing or curse are in the power of the tongue (Proverbs 18:21, Deuteronomy 11:26). Our life and all its issues are a direct result of the things we think and then speak! We are a spirit that possesses a soul and we live in a body (1 Thessalonians 5:23). Our soul is our mind, will, intellect, and emotions. Our body is led by our soul. Our actions are usually based on what we think or the way we feel concerning a situation.

When we ask Jesus into our lives, our spirit gets born again, giving us access to every promise that the Bible offers (John 3:6). We need to educate ourselves by studying God's Word as to what is available to us and how God's promises apply to our lives (2 Timothy 2:15). The Bible says that as a man thinks, so is he (Proverbs 23:7). Where the mind goes, the man follows! If we are not happy with the direction that our lives are going, then we need to change the way we think. Do to our diligence in seeking God according to his Word, we obtain insight and understanding, revealing God's perfect plan for our lives. When we change the way we think, it changes the way we believe, which changes the way we speak, which empowers the promises of God to manifest in our lives!

A great example of this is if we need a job, our old way of thinking was based on the economy and what the world tells us to think. When we renew our mind according to God's Word, we realize that not only is God our provider (Philippians 4:19) but that God makes a way when the world says there is no way (Philippians 2:13-14). Our new way of thinking results in a new way of speaking. Rather than speaking the old way, we now begin to speak God's way over our situation. This empowers us to see the promises of God come to pass in our lives! The Bible says that when we begin to confess God's Word regularly, we will have what we speak. We are literally calling into being the promises of God in our lives (Romans 4:17). When we think according to the Word of God but speak according to the old way of thinking, we only frustrate ourselves because we aren't seeing the results that line up to God's promises (James 1:8). Why? This is called hope deferred (Proverbs 13:12), and the Bible states that it makes the heart sick! The Bible states a double-minded man is unstable in all his ways.

We shouldn't allow what we see to determine our future. We should always stand in faith knowing that all God's promises are "yes" and "amen" (2 Corinthians 1:20). God is not a man that he should lie (Numbers 23:19). We wouldn't plant a seed one day, and the next day expect to pick apples. True growth is a process. Stand firm, trust God, speak his Word, and watch your life become a reflection of his promises. Kim and I love you and are excited to see you experience the fullness of God's promises. Have a super awesome day.

The Significance of Armor

Why do we need to put on the armor of God daily? Armor has a unique purpose; it protects us for being injured. Armor also helps us to effectively accomplish our purpose in Christ Jesus! So let's take a look and see what our armor consist of.

The helmet of salvation is a mind-set of who we are in Christ (Ephesians 6:10-18). We can only utilize the helmet of salvation when we know how to think according to the Word of God. The Bible states that as we think, so are we (Proverbs 23:7). Where the mind goes, the man follows! Knowing who we are and all that has been provided to us through salvation sets the standard and equips us to be proficient in serving Jesus.

The next piece of armor is the breastplate of righteousness. This is to protect our heart! When we guard our heart with all that is righteous, it will keeps us going in the right direction. As a man thinks in his heart, so is he (Proverbs 23:7), and out of the abundance of the heart, the mouth speaks (Luke 6:45).

The third thing on our list is the belt of truth. The Bible states that truth empowers us to be free and allows us to set others free (John 8:32). The Bible also states that we should not put our faith and trust in any man but rather every word that comes from the mouth of God (Psalms 143:6, 118:8). God is the embodiment of truth (John 14:6), and when we wrap his truth around us, it does two things. First, it leads us in the right direction (Psalms 25:5), and second, it empowers us to lead others in truth (Matthew 10:8).

The next piece is the shield of faith. The Bible says that a man without faith is unpleasing to God (Hebrews 11:6). So where do we get faith? The Bible states that faith comes from hearing and applying the Word of God (Romans 10:17)! The greater your understanding of the Word of God, the greater your faith. This kind of faith can move mountains in our lives (Mark 11:22-24). Also the Bible states that the shield of faith protects us from the fiery darts of

The Simplicity of a Practical Jesus

Satan's plans and schemes (Ephesians 6:16). So what is faith? Faith is the substance of things hoped for in the Word of God and the evidence of God's unseen promise (Hebrews 11:1). God said it, I believe it, and the answer is on the way.

The last piece of armor is the shoes of peace. Why peace? Peace gives understanding to God's Word and ensures that God will finish all that he has started in us (Philippians 4:7-8). God's Word is a lamp unto our feet (Psalms 119:105) and states that our footsteps are divinely ordered (Psalms 37:23).

When we combine all these aspects of the Word of God in our lives, we are literally unstoppable (Philippians 4:13). The Bible states that no weapon formed against us will prosper (Isaiah 54:17). God has given us all authority over all principalities and powers of darkness (Ephesians 1:20, Colossians 2:10).

So why isn't there any armor for our backs? Because God never intended us to run from Satan, but rather, Satan should be running from us (Luke 9:62). Kim and I love you. Have a great day!

New Beginnings

We are getting ready to start a new year, and new beginnings are amazing! If you don't have a dream, get one. If you do have one, enlarge it.

The Bible states that there are two reasons God's people perish. One is a lack of knowledge of his Word (Hosea 4:6). The second is a lack of vision (Proverbs 29:18). We can't have vision or purpose without first knowing who we are according to God's Word. Vision is a God-inspired dream of what God can do in us, through us, and for us. God uses our gifts and talents to reach the lost and dying while bringing glory and honor to his holy name. God wants to do the impossible in our lives! We need to draw close to God in the New Year, cultivate a deeper relationship with him, and determine to see God's purpose fulfilled in our lives.

The definition of *insanity* is "doing the same things over and expecting a different outcome." If we don't have a plan for our future, our future will be a repeat of our past. Never forget that our job isn't to find fault or judge anyone (Matthew 7:1-3). We should allow God's love to flow through us, drawing all to come to know and understand the saving grace of Jesus Christ.

The Bible states that the harvest is great, but the workers are few (Matthew 9:37). The only thing we can take to heaven with us is another soul! Know that Kim and I are cheering for you and are super excited to see what amazing things God has in store for your lives in this New Year. Much love and many blessings.

The Simplicity of God

Jesus stated that we should have childlike faith (Matthew 18:2-3). A child believes just because God says so. Children don't have stipulations or need a big explanation; they just believe! Satan wants us to think that God's Word and all that God has for us is complicated and based on works. We often think that when we are bad or miss the mark, God is mad at us, keeping us from talking with our creator. This is nothing more than an attempt to keep us from God's best.

The truth is, God loves us whether we fall or not. The Bible states that a righteous man falls 7 times, but he gets back up (Proverbs 24:16). Jesus forgives us 470 times a day. When we are quick to repent, God is faithful to forgive us our sins (Acts 3:19, 1 John 1:9). God throws our sins as far as the east is from the west, never to remember them again (Psalms 103:12). God forgives and forgets (Hebrews 8:12, Micah 7:19, Isaiah 43:25).

Satan is a liar and knows no truth (John 8:44). When Satan's lips are moving, he is lying. God not only wants great things for our lives but he sent his son to pay the price so that we can have all that God is. We can experience every promise for our lives. God's mercies are new every morning (Lamentations 3:22). The past is gone, and today is a new day. God is for us, and he is excited to fulfill our destiny, giving us the ability to dream big and obtain his purpose for our lives. When it's all God, it is all good. So let go and let God. Have a great day. Kim and I love you and are cheering you on.

The Word Works

When Peter and the rest of the disciples were on the lake in a boat, Peter was the only one who got out of the boat and walked on the water. As long as our thoughts are confined to the boat, we will never accomplish the things that can only be done by getting out of the boat. The words *I can't* should no longer be in our vocabulary! The Bible states, "In Christ, I can do all things" (Philippians 4:13).

Evil can only be overcome by applying the Word of God to our lives. For example, take someone who is trying to change their bad habit of cussing. If they are constantly focused on the problem, stating "I have to quit cussing," the focus is on what they can't do rather what they can! Evil is overcome by the Word, and habits are broken applying the Word. Focus on what you can say, and the bad will fade away.

First things first, let's see what the Bible has to say about my words. It states that life or death is in the tongue (Proverbs 18:21). It also says that my words should be a blessing to myself and others, lifting others up and edifying them (Ephesians 4:29, 1 Thessalonians 5:11). The Bible also instructs us to let no unwholesome word come out of our mouths! So let's put this together and overcome the negative words in our lives with good! Every morning when we get up, say, "Today is the day the Lord has made. I can do all things because he is my strength. I choose to be a blessing with my words today, allowing God to help me not to cuss." Then after you have set the tone for the day, begin to speak good things over and over throughout your day on purpose, allowing the good things you speak to overcome the bad things that you used to speak!

Are you going to be perfect in your attempt to change? No! But remember, a righteous man falls several times, but he gets back up! God's mercies are new every morning. He isn't mad at us; he is mad about us! Okay, so one final thing, don't just change things in your life to say you're a good person, but rather change your life so that you can be a reflection of who Jesus is. People can learn from your example and experience the changing power of Jesus in their lives as well! Nine out of ten times, it's not what you can tell someone about Jesus, it's what you show them through your life that is a reflection of who he is! So read your Bible so that you know what needs to be changed in your life, and strive to put Jesus first in your life. God will do the rest! Kim and I love you and are proud of all of you! You can do it! Have a great day!

The Struggle for Life

I was thinking about bobbing in the middle of the ocean one thousand miles from land in any direction! As I was taking it all in, I realized it's definitely too far to swim. Right off the bat, death is inevitable. I have nothing to eat and ironically no water to drink. There is a huge possibility that a shark will eat me for dinner, I could get stung by a monster jellyfish and spend my last hours on this earth in agony, or I could get eaten by an octopus! Regardless of the situation, my level of fear for the unknown, what, when, or how I will lose my struggle for life, is just as terrifying as the outcome! Then all of a sudden, a cruise ship comes along with dry clothes, great food, a helicopter, and all the amenities needed, not just for a rescue, but a really nice rescue. They pull me out of the water and give whatever they have they offer to me. They don't ask for money, they don't care about my social status, and they are ready to take care of me, relieving my mind of any unknowns. After a great meal, a shower, and some rest and relaxation, you say, "I feel much better now, so if you don't mind, I'm going back into the water. I think I can make it now," that would be the dumbest thing you could ever say. The captain says to you that all what he has can be yours if you just acknowledge his part in your rescue and you do your part to keep the ship clean and help look for others to save along the way. You reply with, "I appreciate the offer, but I got this!"

The ocean is like life without Jesus, just bobbing along, and all the uncertainty of death are the same uncertainties we face in life. The Bible says in and of ourselves we can do nothing, but through Christ, we can do all things (John 5:30). Grace is a funny thing; it's a free gift from God. The only way to experience God's grace is by acknowledging our need for a Savior. The more I walk in God's truth, the greater his grace! The Bible states that the truth will set you free (John 8:32). Truth empowers us to walk in the grace provided through all that was accomplished on the cross! When we get to a place where we feel we no longer need grace and we step back into our old way of thinking and doing, then not only is destruction inevitable but it is certain. I'm not saying sharks won't still try to attack, but we can have comfort that when God is guiding the ship, nothing can destroy us. God promises in his Word that if we stay the course, all things, good or bad, will work out for his glory and our benefit (Romans 8:28).

I recently led a friend to Christ and have been diligent in giving him the truth of how to maintain a beautiful walk with God. God gave him freedom from heroin with no withdrawals. He took him out of a deadend job and blessed him with a job twice the money with unlimited potential for growth. I encouraged him stay in church, read his Bible, and honor God with his money. Now that his life is better and so much more hopeful, he has stopped going to church, stopped feeding his spirit through the Word, and no longer is honoring God with his money. I can see the sharks circling and getting ready to strike, and he just says it's all good! If we could do it on our own, Jesus wouldn't have had to endure his brutal death. The fact is, we do need a Savior! Life will never be something we can conquer on our own! Turn your heart to Jesus, acknowledge him in all you do (Proverbs 3:6), and he will make your paths straight. God has an amazing plan and purpose for your life. When we let go and let God, it is all good! Have a great day. Kim and I love you!

The Walking Dead

I was in the grocery store the other day, and as I sat on the bench waiting for Kim, I began watching all the different types of people as they walked by. I saw a pattern emerging. Many people seemed grumpy, even angry, and very self-centered. The greatest country in the world, yet the majority of the people are unhappy on some level. Most of the people I watched seemed impatient and even annoyed that others were in the checkout line. Impatient with the cashier when having to do a price check. When I went to use the restroom, there was a young boy, maybe fifteen, that was autistic, and the other men in the restroom were very intolerant of his ticks. The sounds he made along with his physical ticks. As one man left the bathroom, he verbalized uneasiness of someone who was different. The woman who was waiting for this boy was angry at the man's disapproval.

I began to ask God to help me process what I was seeing. These people you see are the walking dead! See, the Bible says that Jesus is the way, the truth, and the life (John 14:6) and no man can come to the father except through him. The Bible also states that it's because of all that Jesus accomplished on the cross, we can have an abundant life. The Bible states that we can only have and experience true life through Christ Jesus.

We as a nation have put God out of our schools and out of our government. We have removed him from every aspect of our society, and the life that this country once possessed is now just a faint glimpse of a memory. We have gone from being a nation founded on truth to a nation that cares nothing about others but only ourselves. The walking dead go to and fro day in and day out only concerned of their wants and desires, even if it means using others and hurting those around us.

The Bible states that there is no greater love than a man or woman who would lay their life down for another (John 15:13). No greater love! Today we not only despise that kind of love but we shun the very people who lay their life down for the freedom of our country.

The Simplicity of a Practical Jesus

We have people burning the flag a symbol of our freedom and even defecating on that same flag. We have become a nation of walking dead. God never desired any to perish, but we have traded the truth of God for a lie and we have a form of godli- ness but deny the power thereof. It's never to late to turn our hearts back to God and embrace the very truth that can set us free from the chains of sin and death. Kim and I love you and want God's best for all. Have a great day

The Who and When of Salvation

In John, chapter 4, we see Jesus at the well talking to the Samaritan woman. The Jews of that time saw Samaritans as unclean people and not worthy of God's promises or his provision. The woman at the well had been married five times, and the man she was with currently was not her husband. Not only was she of the wrong race but she was deep in sin. The beauty of all this is Jesus didn't see her for her flaws or problems; he saw the potential for many to come to know and understand his saving grace. Because Jesus took the time to speak with this woman, many in her town experienced salvation.

Many times we look at a person and prequalify them according to what we see and what we think rather than what God sees through his love. Remember, true love, which God is, finds no fault (1 Corinthians 13:5). He only sees potential in what his son accomplished on the cross. The Bible states that it's not God's desire that any man perish but that all should have eternal life (1 Timothy 2:4, 2 Peter 3:9). We as Christians should be a bright reflection of all that Jesus is, allowing the love of God to flow through us, drawing all to come to know and understand the saving grace of Jesus Christ. I know that I have been guilty of this as well. I have looked at some people and thought, *Wow, they are messed up.* In reality, God loves using these kinds of people because it confounds the wise and it is a great display of God's love, mercy, grace, and compassion.

The second issue is timing. Many times we are not dependent on God's timing but what we think. Here is an example. When I had my body shop, there was a man who would often come by to check out our latest projects. He was rough and used lots of profanity and was in no way interested in the things of God. Not too long after he started coming around, I was going to ask him to refrain from using profan- ity in my shop. I quickly heard the Holy Spirit tell me no and then instructed me to just love him. In Romans 8, it states that the love of God through us draws all to a place of understanding so that they can experience salvation. So for a whole year, I took the time to love and encourage this man as he came by my shop. One day he walked in with tears in his eyes, and he stated that every time he walked into my shop, he could feel a warming peace and asked what that was all about. See, because I took the time to love him and see his potential rather than his problems, God brought him to a place of salvation. It took a year to do that, but my timing would have destroyed the opportunity when God's timing was right on time.

In John 4, we see this with the official's son. The Bible states that the boy was healed in the seventh hour, or God's perfect timing. Seven is the number for God's completion, and because it was God's perfect timing, not only was the boy healed, but many came to know and understand all that God had planned for their lives. The Bible states that in and of ourselves, we can do nothing (John 5:30), but through Christ, we can do all things (Philippians 4:13). Let us seek God through reading and applying his Word to our lives and reach as many people as we can. The harvest is plenty, and the workers are few (Matthew 9:37). Kim and I love you and are excited for all that God is doing in you, through you, and for you. Have a great day.

Trust God

The Bible states we should put our faith and trust in no man but rather every word that proceeds out of the mouth of God (Psalms 118:8, 146:3). Kim and I recently experienced a tragic loss. It was literally breathtaking! The enemy took everything near and dear to our heart. We didn't see this attack coming. We never thought in a million years that the people we loved and have spent so many hours encouraging, praying with, and showing the love of God to would play into the enemy's plans and schemes. When the dust settled and Kim and I realized what a huge loss we had suffered, our first question was why. We love God, we are faithful to his Word, and our heart is to see the lost and dying come to know and understand God's saving grace. Why did this happen, God?

This is when you believe that God is who he says he is and that his Word is true, faithful, and just. It's not personal! Don't ever think that you are going to accomplish greatness without opposition. No matter what the situation looks like or how great the loss may be, stay focused! God is in control. God's Word is true, faithful, and just, and his promises are "yes" and "amen" (2 Corinthians 1:20). Just keep doing what you know is right in God's eyes, keep a good attitude, and pray for your accusers. Never forget - truth will always prevail. If we lose everything but still have Jesus, we are golden! It's never for less, but always for more. Kim and I love you and are excited for you to experience all that God has for your life! Have a great day.

3:04 AM

It's September 7, 3:04 a.m., and my mind is going one hundred miles an hour. I have been writing these inspirationals for a couple years now for two reasons. One is to encourage those of you who have Jesus in your heart and are cultivating a closer walk with him. Second is for those who don't know Jesus but realize that there is more to life and are not sure what that is.

The cool thing about either group is that God loves us both the same and has an amazing plan and purpose for each and every one of our lives (Jeremiah 29:11). His mercies are new every morning (Lamentations 3:22-23), and he isn't mad at us but he is mad about us. The importance of having a relationship with the creator of the world isn't just so we can go to heaven, although that's pretty important, but rather so that we can experience a fullness of all that he is and wants to do in our lives. The reason he gives the dos and don'ts in the Word isn't to be controlling; it's for our protection. If we honored God with our relationships and was abstinent prior to marriage and no one engaged in homosexuality, we would literally stop STDs dead in their tracks. If we would honor God with our bodies and wouldn't smoke, drink, or overeat, we could cut out can- cer, liver failure, and heart disease. If we would honor God with our tithe and offerings, not only would we have more than enough, but the churches would be able to provide for the less fortunate.

God's plan was for us is to feed the hungry, not the government. If we would do as the Bible instructs, stating a man who doesn't work shouldn't eat (2 Thessalonians 3:10), we could cut 90 percent of wel- fare! If we would honor God with our decisions, we wouldn't have so many people in prison! If we would honor God by listening to the Bible as it states we owe no man anything but love (Romans 13:8), we wouldn't have so much credit card debt and our nation wouldn't be going broke from reckless spending. The whole of the matter is, God's way leads to health and wholeness physically, mentally, emotionally, and spiritually. It's not about controlling us but prospering us in every area of our lives. One day each and every one of us will stand before God, and we will have to give an account of what we did or didn't do with his Word. God has amazing plans for our lives, but that can only happen if we are walking in truth, honoring him with all that we are. Kim and I are so proud of each and every one of you and want God's best for your lives. God bless and have a great day!

Truth versus a Good Idea

I was watching a movie the other day, and the movie was a love story and about a woman whose husband was murdered. The main premise of the movie is that when good people die, they not only go to heaven but are escorted by angels. When bad people die, they are escorted to hell by demons. There is some truth to this. However, the defining truth was left out. If we want to go on vacation and are going to fly, take a train, or take a bus, we first need to have a ticket. No matter how nice of a person we are, it will not get us on that plain, train, or bus. We would be out of line if we stood there and argued with the airline of what a good person we are while explaining all the great things we have done in our lives. If we persisted, we would find ourselves in jail. Jesus stated that he is the way, the truth, and the life (John 14:6), and no one can come to the father except through him! We have to believe in our hearts and confess with our mouths that Jesus is the son of God (Romans 10:9-10). We need to make Jesus Lord and Savior of our lives! It doesn't matter how good we are. The Bible states we all have sinned and fallen short of the glory of God (Romans 3:23).

Don't get me wrong, I'm not saying the movie was bad, but I am saying that we often watch a good love story like this and never consider that there is more to the story than is being told. This is a great example of programming. We often watch or listen to programming that seems good and harmless, but they are sneaky in misrepresenting truth! When we are bombarded with information and ideas that look like truth but are not truth, it's easy to become confused on what exactly the truth is. The Bible states to renew our minds daily through the washing of the Word (Romans 12:2). It's the Word of God that helps us to define truth and maintain a proper perspective of what is and isn't truth! The problem is if we don't read our Bibles, then the only input we have is misrepresented truth. This makes it easy to lose our way and become powerless to live our lives according to truth. Why? Because the truth sets us free. Not a wrong perspec- tive of truth! No truth, no power. The Bible states that people will trade the truth for a lie (Romans 1:25) and proclaim to know God but deny the power of God. That's why programming is a slippery slope. Please don't hear what I'm not saying. I'm not saying TV and movies are bad, evil, and so forth. I am saying set your heart on the Word of God so that you won't be deceived by something that looks like truth. The definition of brainwashing is a forcible indoctrination to induce someone to give up basic political, social, and religious beliefs or attitudes. Accepting contrasting ideas presented by propa- ganda, salesmanship, or programming. Kim and I love you and are excited for all that God is doing in your lives. Have a great day!

Thy Will Be Done

We can't accomplish what God wants for our lives if we are only willing to do what we want. When my oldest was still a baby, I had the privilege of breaking him off the bottle. He was very determined that he was going to get a bottle. I took the time to put him down for nap, but I was also determined that his bottle days were over. I knew that it was best for my son to give up the bottle because better things were on the horizon.

Many times God has a plan and purpose for our lives and prompts us to do things his way, but most of the time we would rather do it our way because we are comfortable in our current situation. The Bible states that we can do all things through Christ (Philippians 4:13) because he is our strength. However, God requires us to do our part. People often relate their relationship with God with attending church. That is a start, but there is so much more to life than that. Having Jesus in our lives ensures our eternal destination. When we begin to read and apply the Word of God to our lives, we learn to live and experience all that God has for our lives. We are literally empowered to do the impossible. God will only continue to instruct us when we are faithful to do what he shows us.

If you haven't heard from God in a long time, then go back to the last thing he showed you and apply it to your life. God's Word is a river of life that he desires to flow through us. God can't get his best to us if he can't get his Word through us. When we choose to do things our way, we begin to restrict the flow, and if we are not careful, the flow will eventually stop. When the water stops, the drought begins. Drought leaves us thirsty with hopes that one day the rains will come providing water, keeping us from dying of thirst.

The funny thing about drought with God is it doesn't have to be; it's self-inflicted. When we are faithful to follow his instruction and walk in obedience to his Word, he provides the peace of still waters and green pastures for us to enjoy. People often want the green pastures that someone else is enjoying but are not willing to do what they did to experience those green pastures for themselves.

God's Word is amazing, and his promises are "yes" and "amen". God wants to take your willing heart and do amazing things in you, through you, and for you. Always remember God's will isn't just for you but rather so others can experience his faithfulness through you. We are a light in a dark world (Ephesians 5:8). The more we read and apply God's Word to our lives, the brighter the light we become, empowering us to lead others to freedom. Kim and I love you and are excited for all that God has for your life. Have a great day.

Today

Today we celebrate all that was accomplished on the cross. We can literally walk in God's authority and victory. We are empowered to accomplish our purpose in this earth.

The journey of the cross is twofold. First and foremost, it gives us life and redeems us from ever having to go to hell. Jesus paid our debt for sin and gave us eter- nal life. Our journey is just the beginning. The second phase of the cross is to learn how to apply God's love in our lives. Our goal is to draw as many people to the cross as we can. Why? So that they too can come to know and understand the saving grace of all that Jesus accomplished on the cross for them. Jesus himself told us to go into the entire world and bring the truth to all that are lost and dying (Mark 16:15).

One day we will stand before Jesus, and he will ask each and every one of us what we did with all that he accomplished on the cross (Mark 16:15). Will you hear, "Well done. You did an amazing job" (Matthew 25:23)? How many will have escaped death and hell because of your willingness to share the gospel. Learn God's Word and allow his love to shine that all might see. Have a great day. Kim and I love you.

True Balance

Why is balance so important? How is true balance achieved in every area of our lives? Balance can only be achieved when the focal point is dead center. Jesus is that focal point. When our lives are centered on him and his Word is the foundation of our lives, we are empowered to maintain peace, hope, and love in our lives. God's Word brings about harmony in our thoughts, words, and deeds.

The Bible says that as a man thinks in his heart, so is he (Proverbs 23:7), and out of the abundance of the heart, the mouth speaks (Matthew 15:18). We all know that where the mind goes, the man follows. The Bible says to take our thoughts captive so we can weed out the trash that causes us to be imbalanced (2 Corinthians 10:5). When we focus on Jesus, balance is restored. The Bible says that we can put our faith and trust in every word that comes out of God's mouth (Proverbs 30:5, Psalms 146:3).

God instructs us not to worry but to cast our cares on him (1 Peter 5:7). God will provide our needs (Philippians 4:19). God prospers everything we put our hands to do (Deuteronomy 30:9). I can do all things because God is my strength (Philippians 4:13). God is trying to empower us for greatness. In God, there is perfect balance. If we need help achieving balance in our lives, then we should seek God, read his Word, and always be willing to apply whatever he shows us. When we apply God's Word in thought, word, and deed, we will always remain centered in life. The Bible states that in and of ourselves, we can do nothing (John 5:30). Why spend all the time and energy doing what we can't do when we can seek God, where nothing is impossible? Focus and know God has your back! Kim and I love you. We know that in God there are no limits as to what he will do in you, through you, and for you. Have a great day!

True Restoration

Many times I have had people bring me their cars and want me to fix and restore their cars, but only on a cosmetic level. Many times when there is rust that is seen on the outside, there is twice as much rust on the inside that can't be seen. Internal rust opens the door for a lack of structural integrity. Just because something looks good on the outside doesn't mean it isn't a rotten mess on the inside. I have had many people bring me projects that were purchased due to the way the car looked, but on the inside, they were rotten to the core. When doing a restoration, you have to remove 100 percent of the rust before you can begin to build a sound project. There have been instances where I have literally cut 85 percent of all the metal out of a car and started over.

God many times needs to remove cancerous things in our lives in order for true restoration to be achieved. Many times we dress the outside up, but inside we are just a dead man's bones (Matthew 23:27). Maybe our attitude is wrong or our words are destructive. We can only disguise our mess to a certain extent. When we are around a person long enough, the stuff that is on the inside eventually comes out. Worth isn't what we look like on the outside; it's what we are made of on the inside.

When we seek God through reading and applying God's Word to our lives, we begin to remove the garbage that is unappealing to others and basically stinks. As God begins to remove the decay and the rot, we literally become brand-new. The nature of who God is, in all his glory, begins to shine from within, literally making us priceless to those around us. We have the answers in Christ, and we know who and what God intended us to be, leading others in truth and helping them fulfill their destiny in Christ. I have seen many people enter cars that are pretty on the outside to car shows, but then there are those who have the real deal, and not only do their cars bring top dollar but they usually take first place.

When doing any sort of restoration, there is always a cost involved. There is always the need to replace the rotten with something that is good. Don't think that our lives are much different. Many want the fullness of all that God offers, but they are not willing to apply all that is required to see the perfection of God's faithfulness in them. Let's not just be that person who looks like a Christian but is rotting on the inside. Instead, let's embrace all that the Word says we are and all that Jesus accomplished on the cross. We can change this world as we know it one soul at a time. Kim and I love you and want God's best for you. Have a great day.

Truth Requires Change

I was pondering on why so many people are offended by truth. It dawned on me that truth always requires change, and people don't want to change. Jesus said he is the truth (John 14:6). Jesus is also the Word of God in the flesh (John 1:14). The Word of God sets some pretty strong boundaries on what is right and wrong, what is acceptable and what isn't, and who will enter heaven and who won't. Jesus died to remove our sins and to throw them as far as the east is from the west (Psalms 103:12).

We should not continue to walk in sin just because it's what we want. We no longer belong to ourselves. We were purchased with the blood of Christ (1 Corinthians 6:20). Now it is neither our job nor our right to point the finger at or judge anyone (Matthew 7:1-3). We are commissioned by Jesus to disciple in truth and love. I am just pointing out that our determination to seek self-gratification rather than the purity of Christ is causing our nation to reap a harvest of destruction. This is all due to our willingness to step outside the hedge of protection that is available through the obedience to God's Word.

The second issue is we as a nation are no longer standing with Israel. The Bible is very specific that whoever opposes Israel will reap God's wrath (Genesis 12:3). Destruction is inevitable if we do not turn our hearts back to God. I'm not a gloom-and-doom person, but I can see the writing on the wall. Please, if you don't know Jesus as your personal Savior or you knew him at one time but aren't walking with him now, I beg you turn back to him, repent, and seek God for your life. A storm is coming, and it's not something you want to encounter without Jesus in your heart. Look, God loves you and has an amazing plan and purpose for your life, but you have to choose. Choose life! Kim and I love you. Have a great day.

Two Ears and One Mouth

The Bible states that we should listen much and speak little (James 1:19). Why? Have you ever heard someone say actions speak louder than words? People should see our lives as a reflection of all that Jesus is in us rather than the Jesus they hear from us. Today we live in a society that has little to no value on words. Today if someone says they will do something, you have a fifty-fifty chance they will keep their word. This has become normal.

As Christians, our words should be of great value. When we commit to something, we need to keep our word (Proverbs 11:3, 20:25). This builds credibility and provides opportunities to share the gospel. Why? People know your word is golden. I was getting to know someone today, and as I asked them questions about themselves, I made a mental note of their likes and dislikes, their dreams, and what they wanted out of life. Their favorite chili was in Steak 'n Shake. You might ask what all that has to do with the price of eggs in China. How much do you think it would make an impact on this person if I gave them a gift card on their birthday to eat at their favorite restaurant? What kind of impact would it make for them to know I was truly listening?

We should use every opportunity to advance the gospel (Ephesians 5:15). The Bible says it's the love of God through us that draws all people to understand God's goodness and his salvation (Romans 2:4). Take the time to listen while allowing God's love to flow. When the time is right and the Holy Spirit has drawn that person close, preparing their heart for the day of salvation, they will receive openly. Change your world as you know it. Keep Jesus first. The rest is history. Kim and I love you. Have a great day.

Until We Meet Again

Good morning to all our friends that work with Kim. I wanted to take a minute and devote today's inspirational to you guys. Kim came to work with you one and a half years ago. This wasn't even on her list of places to apply, but Kim and I both realized that it's not always about what we want but rather about God's plan and purpose. Kim took this job expecting that as she let her light shine, you might come to know and understand all that God has for your life when putting Jesus first. During her time with you, Kim has done a great job of allowing Jesus to shine in her life, setting the example needed for each and every one of you to know and understand God's amazing love for you.

The time has come for Kim to embrace a new journey, and as she says her goodbyes, don't allow this to be a missed opportunity in your life. Having Jesus in our hearts is more than just having a ticket to heaven; it's about getting to know and experiencing a relationship with the creator of all things. How amazing is that? The key to living a successful life full of all that God promises is your willingness to read and apply the written Word of God—the Bible! Remember, you only get what you put into it. The more you seek God through his Word, the more your life becomes a reflection of God's goodness and his many blessings for your life.

Don't think you can do the minimum and get the maximum. One day we will all stand before our creator, and God will ask us what we did with what he gave us. Always know Kim and I love you. We want great things for your life, and God has amazing plans for your life. Despite what Kim and I want or God's plans, it's up to you whether you see all that he has ensured for your life. We pray that Kim and I have made a difference in your lives, bringing you closer to your creator. We will continue to pray for you and your journey. We love you and are grateful that God has blessed our lives with the opportunity to get to know each and every one of you. Much love and many blessings, Kirk and Kim.

Using Every Opportunity

Today I got a roommate that needs dialysis for kidney failure. His addiction to crack cocaine has contributed to his kidney issues. I had offered to pray for him, and he declined sharply. The Bible says that it's God's love through us that draw all to a place of understanding while experiencing all that Jesus accomplished on the cross for us (Romans 2:4). I offered my roommate some snacks, candies, chips, and cookies, things people had brought me in gift baskets. After a few minutes, he said, "I'm sorry, I was so abrupt earlier. You can pray for me if you still want to." I dragged myself from my hospital bed teetering while struggling to use my walker and slowly shuffled over to his bed. I began to explain to him how much God loves him. This man began to tell me that God was mad at him for his addiction and many failures. I assured him that God was not mad at him, but rather God was mad about him. I continued to explain that God has so many good things in store for him, and I prayed. The man thanked me for not being mad at his rude behavior.

Later that day the lady from physical therapy came to see me. I simply asked her if she had ever taken the time to ask Jesus into her heart. I explained she was created for fellowship with the creator of all things. I went on to state not only was she destined for salvation but that God had amazing plans and purpose for her life. She said, "You know, you're the second person today to share faith with me." I told her that God loved her so much and desired a relationship with her that he sent two different people into her life so she could experience all that God has for her life.

Everyone needs to be loved, and without us sharing that love and God's truth, they are literally hell bound. God has entrusted us with other people's souls! Allow God to use you today to touch someone else's life. Kim and I love you. Have a great day.

What Pleases God?

The Bible states that a man without faith is unpleasing to God (Hebrews 11:6). This is a profound statement. What is it about faith that is so important to out creator? Where does faith come from? From reading and applying the Word of God to our lives (Romans 10:17). Why?

The Word of God is the key that unlocks the total power of God in any situation. When the spirit of God was hovering over the water and the earth was a dark void and without form, it was his Word that changed the circumstance (Genesis 1:1). God spoke, and there was light. The same Word of God that spoke everything into existence is the same Word that is given to us to accomplish everything that God has for us.

The other day I lost my job and I am faced with a fork in the road. I can look at the problem, or I can speak God's Word over my problem and watch God work in my behalf. The Word states that he is my provider (Philippians 4:19), he makes a way when there is no way (Isaiah 43:16-19), he gives me favor with all the right people, he states that all things (good or bad) work together for my good because I love him and are called according to his purpose (Romans 8:28), and my footsteps are divinely ordered (Psalms 119:133). See, God invested his son, and God watches over his Word to perform it. So as I stand on his Word, faith grows in my heart, and my problem becomes subject to the power of God's Word, bringing to pass the promises of my creator, God himself. How beautiful is that?

If you are faced with problems today, I encourage you to find out what God's Word says about your problem, and walk in the amazing power of his Word because God is not a respecter of persons. What he does for me, he will do for you. Kim and I love you. Have a great day.

What Defines You?

Who or what defines you? Some people feel that money, cars, status, friends, clothes, their job, the size of their house, and on and on determine who they are and what they are worth. We have all met someone in our lifetime that thinks they are someone due to their understanding of the things that define them in life.

The bad part of putting your worth in temporary things is that tomorrow is not guaranteed to anyone and things and status can easily be taken or lost (Proverbs 27). We don't need things to tell us what God has already told us. We are the apple of his eye (Zechariah 2:8), a royal priesthood (1 Peter 2:9), and when our lives reflect God's nature; we are givers, compassionate, considerate, and mindful of others; and we allow the goodness of God to shine through us, then we are truly defined. Miracles of God's promises begin to be evident in our lives. He prospers everything we put our hands to (Deuteronomy 30:9), he makes a way where there is no way (Philippians 2:13, Isaiah 43:16-19), he gives us favor—his promises are endless.

Don't allow yourself to be fooled. In and of ourselves, we are nothing (2 Corinthians 3:5), but through God, all things are possible (Matthew 19:26). Allow God's love to guide you, and everything else are just perks! Kim and I love you and are excited for all that God wants to do in you, through you, and for you. Have a great day!

What Does Your Insurance Plan Look Like?

There are many types of insurance plans that are available in our lives. Every insurance plan has a premium or what it costs us. Plans range from total restoration of any loss while other plans require a deductible. A deductible usually results in a lower premium but require we pay more before our insurance actually provides restoration. The only thing better than having 100 percent coverage with no deduct- ible is someone else paying the premium. Everyone wants this plan. Why? This type of plan is the best peace of mind we can have. It's free and 100 percent. What about the person who doesn't have any insurance? These people always have a cloud over their head ready to burst with storms with no hope of safety.

The beauty of bowing to the lordship of Jesus Christ and allowing God's Word to guide us in life ensures us that when adversity comes, God will turn the situation around for his glory and our benefit (Romans 8:28). God's insurance plan states that even when Satan tries to bring destruction, we always come out on top. God's plan provides for health and wholeness mentally, physically, and spiritually. God provides peace of mind when others have no hope (Philippians 4:7). God provides for our needs, filling them by his means (Philippians 4:19). God lavishes us with thousands of promises that are nothing short of God's amazing love for our lives.

If this is all true and this plan is provided because of what Jesus accomplished on the cross rather than our own efforts, then why doesn't everyone have this plan? The world offers nothing but heartache, loss, struggle, and no hope in this life or the life to come. Although the plan is free, God still requires us to accept his plan, allowing him to become the reflection of his faithfulness in our lives. Don't just have the insurance plan that allows you the peace of mind of spending eternity in heaven while struggling in this life. Allow God to become all that he has promised, giving you an amazing experience while on this earth as well. God empowers us for greatness while achieving the impossible. Nothing is impossible when God is in control (Luke 1:37). Let go and let God, because when it's all God, it's all good. Kim and I love you and want great things for your life. Have a great day.

What Kind of Tree Are You?

The difference between a nonbearing peach tree and a bearing peach tree is the nonbearing looks like a peach tree but has no fruit to provide nourishment. A bearing tree produces fruit that can give nourishment to whoever eats of it! The Bible states that we are known by the fruit we bear (Matthew 7:16).

So what does it mean to bear good fruit? The Bible states that life and death are in the power of the tongue (Proverbs 18:21). Life being God's way versus death being humanity's way! So the Bible says we should renew our minds daily (Romans 2:12). Why? As long as we think wrong, we will continue to speak wrong, and our lives will be a reflection of our wrong way of thinking, meaning man's way of thinking. God states that our way of thinking is not his way of thinking, so in order to think like God, we need to renew our minds (Isaiah 55:8-9). The Bible states as we think, so are we (Proverbs 23:7), and out of the abundance of the heart, the mouth speaks (Matthew 15:18). And this means what? We might say that we believe that Jesus provided healing when he took the thirty-nine lashes on his back, but if we only speak things contrary to the truth, then our situation is going to be a reflection of our words!

For example, the doctor says I am terminal. My friend had the same thing and died from it. There is no cure. These words will only bring death. But if we change the way we think to the way God thinks and we speak life rather than death, it literally allows God to work in our behalf. We should speak life, such as by his stripes, we are healed (Isaiah 53:5), Jesus came to give us life and the abundance of life (John 10:10), and with a long life, Jesus will satisfy us (Psalms 91:16).

As we speak life, then our lives will become a reflection of the lifegiving words we speak out of our mouths. For example, the Bible states that salvation was provided by the death, burial, and resurrection of Jesus, but in order to experience that truth, we have to realize our need for a Savior. Only then can we believe in our hearts and confess with our mouths that Jesus is Lord and salvation takes place in our lives (Romans 10:9). In the same way as we renew our minds through the Word, we can believe in our hearts that all God's prom- ises are "yes" and "amen" (2 Corinthians 1:20). As we begin to speak life, then our lives begin to reflect the promises of God. The Bible says that we will be known by the fruit we bear (Matthew 7:16). If we confess we are Christians but have no fruit, then our Christianity is no different than that of a nonbearing fruit tree. With no fruit, we have nothing to offer anyone.

Jesus traded his deity to take on humanity. As Jesus spent time seeking the Father through prayer and fellowship, his words were a reflection of all that the Father is. Jesus produced fruit that validated who the Father was in his life. Jesus stated, "If you have seen me, you have see the Father, because the Father and I are one" (John 14:9). The Bible states that we are the righteousness of God through Christ, so as we renew our minds and believe in our hearts confessing with our mouths, our lives become a reflection of who Jesus is (Romans 3:22, 2 Corinthians 5:21).

We as Christians should be able to say, "If you have seen me, you have seen Jesus, for Jesus and I are one." The fruit that we bear in our lives gives proof that we are the righteousness of God in Christ. If we truly want to walk in all that God has for us and we want to fulfill all God's plans for us, then it's simple: read your Bible. We can only know what and who we are in Christ when we read and apply God's Word to our lives. When we believe in our hearts that what he says in his Word is true and begin to speak God's truth rather than man's truth, then our lives will become the perfect reflection of all that Jesus is in us. We will lay hands on the sick and watch them heal. We will be able to cast out devils and set the captive free. We will live a life of power and victory rather than a life of defeat and despair, keeping us from experiencing all that God has for us. Kim and I love you and are excited for all that God is doing in you, through you, and for you. Have a great day!

What to Do?

We often find ourselves in situations, and we just don't know what to do. We want to make right decisions, but we just aren't sure what they are. Kim and I are kind of in that spot now on where to move. We know that we aren't supposed to be where we are currently at. We have looked at several places, and a couple of them we really like. In praying and seeking God on what to do, we prayed that God's will will be done while thanking him that our footsteps are divinely ordered (Psalms 37:23) and that he makes a way where there seems to be no way (Isaiah 43:16-19). When we pray, we ask that if one wasn't right, he would close that door and keep us from walking through it. We also ask that the right door would be open wide with no misunderstanding.

Kim likes a particular house and really wants it bad. She is willing to allow God to open or close that door. Why? Because she knows that if God says no, it just means he sees something we don't and that he has something better in store. It's never for less; it's always for more!

When we set ourselves on the Word of God and seek his ways versus our desires, it will always work out in our favor. In Psalms 119, it states that his Word is a lamp unto our feet and a light unto our path. In Joshua 1:8, it states I will meditate on the Word of God day and night that I may observe and do according to all that it instructs me to do, for then the Lord will make my way prosperous, and then I will deal wisely and have great success! This not only takes us where we need to go, giving us the best situation, but safeguards our lives from heartache and setbacks. Everything that pertains to living our life to the fullest can be found and applied in the Word of God. Kim and I love you and are excited for all that God has in store for your lives. Have a super awesome day.

When Satan Tries to Discredit Us

The Bible states that we wrestle not against flesh and blood but against principalities and powers of darkness (Ephesians 6:12). When someone rises against us in what they say, the Bible states that every tongue that rises against us in judgment shall be proved to be in the wrong (Isaiah 54:17). How?

Well, first of all, we need to realize that Jesus is in us and Jesus is greater than the one who is lying. Second, the truth always comes out. The Bible states that no matter what the enemy does or says, if we will trust God, he will turn the situation around for his glory and our benefit (Romans 8:28). We should always allow our lives to be a reflection of Jesus, continuing to let our light shine. Choose to walk in love, allowing God to work in our behalf. Hurting people hurt people! We should never allow offense to take space in our hearts (Proverbs 11:19, Luke 17). We should pray for our enemies, allowing God to reveal the truth (Luke 6:28).

The truth isn't just for our benefit, but it reveals the power of God working in our lives and draws others to the saving grace of Jesus Christ. Satan's goal is to cause division. The Bible states that a house divided can't stand (Mark 3:25). Division keeps the healing power of God from operating in all lives involved. People are not the problem. It's never personal! Satan uses people as pawns to do his bidding. Satan hates everyone involved and wants to bring destruction to all. Keep Jesus first, and rest in knowing that God is in control. Kim and I love you and want the very best for you! Have a great day.

When Taking a Test

Life is full of many lessons. When we have finished the lesson, we learn we'll always have a test. The only time we have to retake a test is when we fail it. When we were in school, we were given every tool needed to ace our test. Some of us never even opened our books but were surprised when we failed. Some of us were half-hearted in our studies and okay with just getting by. Some of us embraced the books and learned all we could while achieving success when testing. Now if the slacker were to say it just doesn't work for everyone, we would say no, you just didn't apply yourself!

The Bible stands for basic instruction before leaving earth. Every aspect of our lives is covered in the Word of God. When we take the time to study, we can achieve success and move on to the next lesson. A lot of times we seem to go through the same things over and over, never really moving forward in our lives. Why? We don't take the time to seek God's wisdom concerning our lives. We just keep taking the test without reading the lesson plan and failing over and over again. So how do we achieve success in every area of our lives? By studying the book!

The Bible states that we should renew our minds daily through the washing of the Word (Ephesians 5:26, Romans 12:2). All the answers are in the book! We just need to do our part. We can be powerful or pitiful, succeed or fail, the choice is ours. The only person who determines the outcome is us. We need to read our Bibles daily and ask God to give us insight and understanding. We will literally become a reflection of all that Jesus is and all that he accomplished on the cross, changing our lives and the lives around us forever. Kim and I love you and want great things for your lives. Have a great day, and know that we love you and are cheering for you.

When the Flow Stops

I recently lost my job, and my routine has changed. As I am at home and not interacting with people, it is real easy to get complacent in my walk with God. The Bible states that we should renew our minds daily through reading and applying the Word of God to our lives (Romans 12:2, Ephesians 4:23). However, this is not enough. I need faith and works for an even balance in my relationship with God and man (James 2:14-26). The last thing Jesus commanded as he was ascending to heaven was, "Go into the world and make disciples of all" (Mark 16:15). This is the works part of my relationship with God. Each one of us has been given a gifting and ability. These giftings are God's way of taking his Word and funneling it through our lives, allowing us to reach the lost and dying in the lives around us on a daily basis. My gifting is the ability to write and communicate the Word of God while encouraging others to fulfill their destiny in Christ and their purpose in this earth.

The other day I was being bombarded with wrong thoughts and temptations of things I haven't experienced in a long time. At first I just thought okay, well, this is just a scheme of the enemy, and I just need to resist him. As the days passed by, the temptation and thoughts became stronger. I asked God why this was, and here is the response I got. As I became complacent and quit sharing the Word of God in writing my inspirationals, the flow of the Word stopped in my life, and I became stagnant.

If God can't get it through you, then he can't get it to you. As I give into the lives of others, he replenishes what I'm giving out, and there is a flow of living water in my life (Luke 6:38). I allowed the flow to stop, and my life was no longer a source that God was using to reach and love those around me. Many times people get saved and don't educate themselves with the Word of God. They have enough of God to stay out of hell, but not enough to have victory in their lives. We are all called to work. The Bible states that the harvest of souls is many, but the workers are few (Luke 10:2). Keep in mind that works without faith is dead (James 2:14- 26). Faith comes from the Word of God (Romans 10:17).

As we seek God daily in his Word and we begin to apply his Word to our lives, then the miracle begins. Streams of living water begin to flow through us, and our lives become complete (John 7:37- 39). Why? The Bible states that God's people die spiritually for two reasons: a lack of knowing his Word and a lack of purpose or vision (Hosea 4:6, Proverbs 29:18).

When we read the Word daily, faith grows in our hearts, and our works are literally empowered through all that Christ accomplished on the cross, and we can change the world around us as we know it. So as I seek God today and allow his love to flow through me, I am able to encourage you so that you too can fulfill your purpose in this earth. The Bible states that we should freely give because it has been freely given to us (1 Corinthians 2:12, Matthew 10:8). What has been freely given? Truth! It's the truth or the Word of God in us and through us that sets the captives free (John 8:32). God in truth sets us free. Free from what? A wrong way of thinking! The Bible states that where the mind goes, the man follows, and as a man thinks in his heart, so is he (Proverbs 23:7). That's why we need to renew our minds daily, allowing the Word of God to wash the grime of wrong thinking from us (Ephesians 5:26). In return, we need to allow God's Word to flow through us to give free- dom to those around us. Kim and I love you and are excited for all that God is doing in you, through you, and for you. Have a great day.

When the Word Goes from Our Head to Our Heart

Having head knowledge of God's Word but not heart knowledge is like having a gun that isn't loaded. The gun gives the appearance of power, but when it comes down to it, the power is nothing more than an illusion. Many times we read and learn the Word of God only to say we know it in our mind, but because we don't apply truth in our hearts, it is powerless to deliver us from the plans and schemes of the enemy. Satan knows the Word of God forward and backward, but he will never walk in the provision of all that is available in the Word because salvation is a heart issue, not a head issue. In John, chapter 5, we see several examples of people with head knowledge. Jesus even made the comment that truth didn't dwell in them, meaning they had not allowed their hearts to be changed by what they knew.

The first person Jesus encountered was the man at the pool of Bethesda. The Bible states that this man had been lying there for thirty-eight years waiting for someone to put him in the water when it would stir (John 5:1-15). Jesus asked the man, "Do you really want to be healed?" I would think that in thirty-eight years he would have been able to inch his way in to the water to receive his healing. But this guy lived with his affliction because his knowledge never took action. He was waiting for someone else to do it for him. Jesus told the man, "Pick up your mat and walk." The miracle didn't happen when it was spoken; it happened when the man acted on the words of Jesus. How many times are we equipped with the power of the Word, but because we don't act on the Word, we remain powerless?

The second situation was with the religious leaders of the day. Their heads were full of knowledge, but again it was a stumbling block. They were so engrossed with the rules they were not able to acknowledge the miracle of the Word. The amazing part of this story is we are still engrossed in rules and denying the power of the truth to this day. The church has so many different denominations, and all have their rules of how God works and who can access that power. The truth is simple.

Read your Bible, apply God's Word, walk in love, let your light shine, and be the reflection of all that Jesus is and all that he accomplished on the cross. When we allow the Word to manifest in our hearts and renew our minds, transforming the way we think, then we will experience all that God wants to do in us, through us, and for us. Kim and I love you. Have a great day.

When the Rubber Meets the Road_____

Being a Christian is more than just having Jesus in our heart. Christianity is about learning to hear the voice of God while walking in submission to his Word. It's all about relationship. I'm not sure why our human nature is so set on doing what we think and what we want versus what God wants. God always has our best interest at heart. If God asks us to give something up, it's because he has something better for us in mind. It's never for less; it's always for more. When we don't listen to what God is telling us, things begin to fall apart, times get tough, and we begin to hate life. When we walk in our own strength, we set ourselves up for disaster and disappointments (John 5:30).

Get to know God's voice by reading his Word (John 10:27). When we hear God's voice, we should be quick to say "Yes, Lord" and do what he asks. When we live life in and of our own strength, we limit our abilities for greatness. The best we can do is average. When we do it through the strength of God's Word and the calling of his voice, the sky is the limit. God makes a way where there is no way empowering us to do all things in Christ (Isaiah 43:16-19, Philippians 2:13). We are no longer limited financially, spiritually, emotionally, and so forth. Literally life becomes limitless.

Obedience is the catalyst for success. People don't want to follow us because we know the right answers. People will follow us because the right answers in God's Word applied produces success or fruit of his faithfulness! So let's go and show the world what God can accomplish when we are willing, or the rubber meets the road. Kim and I love you and are excited for your success in Christ! Let's change the world as we know it. Have a great day.

Which Way Are You Going?

I was on my way to work today and noticed that the traffic going the opposite direction was backed up for miles. People fighting the day-to-day grind of bumper-to-bumper traffic. I noticed that there were just five or six people on my side of the highway. We were going the opposite direction of the chaotic mess of morning traffic. The Bible states that it is not God's desire for any many to perish but for all to have eternal life (2 Peter 3:9). The Bible also states that many are called and few are chosen (Matthew 22:14). God has an amazing plan and purpose for each and every one of our lives and has called all of us to know and understand these plans that he has for us (Jeremiah 29:11). In order for us to experience all of God's best, he first requires us to bow our knees to the lordship of Jesus Christ. When we walk in the direction of his mighty Word, we allow all that God is to permeate our lives. When we choose the road less traveled, we experience the freedom of God's amazing plan (Matthew 7:13). This allows us to go a new direction in our lives, while everyone else seems to be stuck going the wrong direction. Following the masses limits us and binds us to the flow and same direction of everyone else. The benefits of going the opposite direction are many.

Okay, so please don't hear what I'm not saying. I am not saying that just because we have more freedom on the path that gives life, we won't encounter problems. I am saying that when we do choose God's way, we are equipped to have the peace of God in our lives, and his Word directs us through the troubles that life presents (Psalms 119:05). God's Word empowers us to overcome any plan or accident from time to time or even road construction occasionally on the road of life. We, however, are no longer stuck in the same bumper-to-bumper mess that most people choose to endure in life.

Life without Jesus is limited, with no hope of anything better. God's way requires us to think outside the box, but the benefits far outweigh the hopelessness that the world is stuck with. The Bible states that God has set before us two paths (Deuteronomy 33:15-20).

One leads to death and separation from God's best, while the other is full of life. A life guided by God is full of perks that enrich our relation- ship with our creator. Just so there is no confusion on which road to choose, God says choose the road that leads to life.

Kim and I love you and are excited for you to experience God's best for your lives. Have a great dayscheme that Satan might throw in our direction. We might encounter an accident from time to time or even road construction occasionally on the road of life. We, however, are no longer stuck in the same bumper-to-bumper mess that most people choose to endure in life. Life without Jesus is limited, with no hope of anything better. God's way requires us to think outside the box, but the benefits far outweigh the hopelessness that the world is stuck with. The Bible states that God has set before us two paths (Deuteronomy 33:15-20). One leads to death and separation from God's best, while the other is full of life. A life guided by God is full of perks that enrich our relation- ship with our creator. Just so there is no confusion on which road to choose, God says choose the road that leads to life. Kim and I love you and are excited for you to experience God's best for your lives. Have a great day

The ABC's of Spiritual Warfare

First things first, always walk in love. Why? Because love conquers all (1 Peter 4:8). God is love—it's not a character trait; it is who he is! John 1:1 states that in the beginning was the Word; the Word was with God, and the Word was God! Jesus is the Word made flesh (John 1:14). Jesus is love. So when Jesus is in us, then people should see his love in us and through us. When we allow Jesus to permeate our lives, we can conquer anything. The Bible states that we can do all things through Christ because he is our strength (Philippians 4:13). Love conquers all (1 Corinthians 13). In him, we are empowered for greatness. Jesus states that we would do even greater things than he did (John 14:12).

The next thing is stop randomly asking and start thanking. Jesus has given us every tool needed to accom- plish anything in our lives. The last thing Jesus said on the cross was, "It is finished" (John 19:30), meaning there was nothing more to do. We need to stop randomly asking and find out what God has to say about our situation in the Word. We need to speak the answer rather than the problem. The difference between having a victim mentality and an overcoming mentality is the Word of God. For example, we need a job, but we don't ask God to provide a job. The Bible says that if a man doesn't work, he doesn't eat (2 Thessalonians 3:10). The Bible states that God will provide all our needs according to his riches in Christ Jesus (Philippians 4:19). God makes a way where there is no way (Philippians 2:13). This then is how we should pray:

> Father God, I thank you for your Word that is true, faith-
> ful, and just. I thank you that your promises are "yes"
> and "amen" [2 Corinthians 1:20]. I thank you that
> everything I put my hands to will prosper
> [Deuteronomy 28:8]. I thank you that you give me favor
> with all the right people [Proverbs 3:4]. I thank you that
> my footsteps are divinely ordered [Psalms 37:23]. I

thank you for all that you are doing in me, through me, and for me. Thank you for the perfect job, amen!

This is an effective prayer. Why? God states in his Word that when we pray according to his Word, he not only hears our prayers but he answers them (1 John 5:14). God watches over his Word to perform it (Jeremiah 1:12). God's Word will not return void; it will accomplish all it was sent to do (Isaiah 55:11). God instructs us to call those things that are not as though they are (Romans 4:17). For example, God is the same yesterday, today, and forevermore (Hebrews 13:8), and he gives us an example of calling into existence using the creative ability of our tongue. In Genesis 1:1, it states that the spirit of God hovered over the water. The earth was dark and without form. God never acknowledged the problem. It was dark. God only spoke the answer. God said, "Let there be light," and the problem went away! He spoke, and his word changed the problem.

We were created in God's image (Genesis 1:27). God instructs us to speak the Word over our problems, and we can see the same results (Mark 11:23). Call those things that are not as though they are. When we speak God's Word over the problem, need, or concern, God's Word will overcome and change the circumstance. The importance of knowing God's Word is so that we are equipped to accomplish anything! The next step is knowing the authority that Jesus gave us in his death, burial, and resurrection. The Bible states that whatever we bind on earth is bound in heaven and whatever is lost on earth is lost in heaven (Matthew 18:18). We have been given all authority over all principalities and powers of darkness (Ephesian 1:21). Also it's important to realize that when we pray in secret, we will be rewarded openly (Matthew 6:6). What is the reward? The answer to your prayer. So let's give an example. Say you have a friend named Jimmy Joe, and he has anger issues and struggles with depression. This is how you should pray:

The Simplicity of a Practical Jesus

Father, I thank you for your faithfulness. I thank you for rewarding me openly for my willingness to pray in secret. I thank you that you have given me authority over all principalities, and I bind every spirit that is keeping Jimmy Joe in a place of deception and bondage to Satan's lies. I lose Jimmy Joe to receive from the Holy Spirit and the ministering angels, and I thank you that it's not your desire that any man perish. I thank you that you desire Jimmy Joe to know and understand your love, your mercy, and your compassion. I thank you for bringing other Christians into Jimmy's life to love him and to never judge him but draw him to a place of repentance. Thank you for fulfilling your purpose in Jimmy's life. I love you and praise you. In Jesus's name, amen!

The Bible says that a man without faith is unpleasing to God. What is the opposite of faith? Fear! Fear is the counterfeit of faith! Faith brings God's promise to fruition, and fear allows the enemy access to our lives, giving Satan the right to bring whatever we fear to reality (Hebrews 11:6). So where does faith come from? From reading and applying the Word of God (Romans 10:17). If you read the book of Job, we have an example of the power of fear! Job stated that the things he had feared most had come to pass (Job 3:25). It literally gave Satan access to Job's life. We never want to pray, "God, if it be your will." Why? Because the Bible says to study to show yourself approved. Meaning, the answers are in the Word. We need to read it and study it. When we need it, we are literally empowered to overcome or show ourselves approved! God has an awesome plan and purpose for your life, and I'm so excited to be able to share these things with you. Kim and I love you and are rooting for you.

If Today Was Your Last

The Bible states that we should live our lives as if today is our last but plan as if we have eternity (Ecclesiastes 9:1-12). So the big question is this, if you knew that at the end of the day you would stand before your creator, what would you do differently today? I have been thinking about this for a couple of days now. Is there anyone in your life that you would need to forgive? Is there anyone you would want to say "I love you" to? Would it matter that someone cut you off in traffic or was rude to you at work? Would you let sin interfere with your last day on this earth knowing that in just a few short hours you will stand before Jesus? What would you do differently?

Okay, so let's look at the flip side. If we are supposed to live our lives as if we have eternity, then would we have the same carefree attitude in dealing with life? Would we allow Satan to steal our joy, kill our love, and destroy our purpose in this earth? The reason Satan wants our joy is because the joy of the Lord is our strength. He wants to kill our love, because without love, we can accomplish nothing. He wants to destroy our purpose because our purpose in Christ is to love people while giving them hope that they to can come to know and understand the saving grace of Jesus Christ. With no joy, love, or purpose, we are just merely existing. We wouldn't invite a thief into our house, but oftentimes we allow Satan to steal everything that God intended for us to live an abundant life.

The Bible states that tomorrow is promised to no one (Matthew 6:34). So as we start our day, let's live our lives as if we are going to see Jesus. Let's live a life of purpose knowing that every day we live with purpose and we are making an eternal impact on those around us. Lives will be healed, our words can bring hope, God's love through us draws all men to know and understand the saving grace of Jesus Christ, and when we do stand before Jesus, he will say, "Well done, good and faithful servant" (Matthew 25:23). So as you begin your day, know that you have a purpose, and if you are willing to let go and let God, then you will make an eternal difference. Kim and I love you. Have a great day.

The Art of Giving

The greatest challenge in the Christian faith is a willingness to give. Why is this so important? When God created us, he created us in his image (Genesis 1:27). That means what? This means we should be a reflection of who God is! What was the very first thing God did before anything was created? He gave (1 Peter 1:20). The Bible states that before the foundations of the world, God gave his son Jesus to be slain for our sins. God's first gift was his son. That is epic! Look at the return on his investment. He gave his son, and in doing so, he gained many sons and daughters.

See, Satan doesn't want us to be givers because he knows that first of all when we do, we are perfect reflections of who God is. Also when we give, it gives God the ability to bless our giving. God takes our little. He multiplies it and gives it back up to a hundredfold. God doesn't need our money; he wants our heart. We are stewards. There is a big difference between being an owner of something and being a steward of something. If it were not for God, we wouldn't even be alive and have the ability to make money. But pride says, "I earned this money." In reality, God gives us divine opportunities and prospers our efforts. It is ludicrous to think we have what we have due to our own strength.

On another note, the Bible states that the love of God through us draws all to the understanding of who God is and what he has for all who embrace his gift (Romans 2:4)—Jesus! The Bible also states that if we see someone in need and can meet that need but don't help, the love of God is not in us (1 John 4:7-21). I realize there are a lot of variables to this and that we can't fix or provide for everyone, but if we will seek God and ask him to guide us and be willing to do as he instructs us, then our lives will be full of purpose, and many will come to know and understand the salvation that God has for them. Always realize the only thing we can take to heaven with us is another soul. That makes souls the highest commodity in all of heaven and earth! For example, when God blesses me with a new car, I always give my old one to someone who doesn't have one. Not only am I meeting someone's need, but I am using the opportunity to show God's love. Love conquers all. Sowing is always greater than the sale. The sale is limited to the price of the sale, but the seed is limitless to what God can do through me. Live your life on purpose, allowing God to fulfill his purpose in your life. Your life will literally reach many, making an impact on their lives for the greater good of the gospel. Kim and I love you. Have a great day!

The Brighter Light

Last night I was getting up for my nightly trip to the restroom, and as I sat on the edge of the bed, I was looking at my vision board. I could just barely see the outline of the vision when I thought if there were more light, I could see this better. As I was walking to the restroom, the Lord reminded me that Jesus is the light of the world (John 8:12). I then realized that the brighter Jesus shines in my life, the clearer my vision becomes not just to me but to those around me. When our lives become a clear reflection of who Jesus is, we are literally empowered to accomplish anything. When our attitude is good in times of distress, when we treat people good even when they are not good to us, it opens the door for God to be able to do amazing extraordinary things in us, through us, and for us.

You might ask what a vision is. A vision is a dream inspired by God that allows us to use our gifts and talents to reach people for his glory. My gifting would be anything creative and an ability to communicate. There are so many people that are lost and dying, and we might be the only Jesus they ever see. Allow God to take your ordinary and mix it with his extra, giving us the opportunity for an extraordinary life. Kim and I love you and are excited for you to experience God's fullness. Have a great day.

The Common Denominator

.Do you realize that every success and every failure in life both have the same common denominator? The way we think! The Bible states that as a man thinks, so is he (Proverbs 23:7). This is why the Bible instructs us to renew our minds daily through reading and applying the Word of God in our lives (Romans 12:2). We are also instructed not to hang out with people who are not equally yoked or have the same way of thinking (1 Corinthians 15:33); their ways will become our ways. Bad company corrupts good morals. The only reason they are bad company is because their way of thinking allows for things in their lives that are contrary to the Word of God. The Bible states that through Christ, I can do all things (Philippians 4:13). If I truly believe this, then no one or nothing can keep me from striving for God's best in my life.

When we don't take the time to read our Bibles, we miss out on God's best for our lives. Ignorance does not know what is available through his Word or even how to experience the fullness of God's faithfulness in our lives. When we think of defeat or failure, we often surround ourselves with people that share the same ideas. We find ourselves always wanting better but never able to achieve better. It's like always within reach but never attainable.

When we fail, we often say, "It must not be God's will for my life." When we know who we are in Christ and all that he accomplished for us on the cross, we understand that no matter what Satan uses to bring destruction or despair in our lives, God will turn it around for his glory and our benefit (Romans 8:28).

I quit smoking four years ago. If I sat and thought over and over I'm craving a cigarette, I would eventually give in and smoke. If I placed myself in a room with a bunch of smokers and they said they could never quit and they didn't know how I could, then I would smoke. Instead I quit putting myself in those situations, and when temptation came, I took my thoughts captive as the Word instructs and confessed that in Christ, I can do anything. The more I stepped in the

179

right direction in my thoughts, the easier it became in the flesh. As a man thinks, so is he (Proverbs 23:7).

We can only have God's best when we seek his best. The Bible states that when we seek first the kingdom in   all we think, say, and do, then everything else will be given to us (Matthew 6:33). Everything being just that, deliverance, provision, healing, purpose, destiny, and so on. When we think right, we will speak right, and when we speak right, our lives will be a reflection   of his faithfulness. As a man thinks in his heart, so is he (Proverbs 23:7). Out of the abundance of the heart, the mouth speaks (Luke 6:45). The issues of life flow out of the heart (Proverbs 4:23). Where the mind goes, the man follows. Kim and I love you and are excited for you to experience all that God has for your life. Have a great day.

The Disciple Had a Plan, But Jesus Knew His Purpose

In John, chapter 7, the disciples wanted Jesus to go public with his miracles because they had a plan to see Jesus set up his kingdom on this earth, overthrow the Romans, while restoring Israel to its former glory. The disciples were looking at things in the natural. Jesus came to set the captives free spiritually (Luke 4:18). He came to bring healing to all who needed it. Jesus's purpose far outweighed their plan. Jesus went on to say that when we do the work of the Father, the work we do is real and purposeful, but when we work to promote ourselves and our plan, we are fake and without power. The Bible states that in and of ourselves, we can accomplish nothing (2 Corinthians 3:5), but rather in Christ, we can do all things (Philippians 4:13). Many times we look at life trying to come up with a plan based on circumstance and a worldly knowledge. This sort of plan only leads to a bigger issue and leaves us frustrated and always seeking another answer. The Bible states that when we work in secret, then God will reward us openly (Matthew 6:4).

I had a job, and I went above and beyond every day while doing my job unto God. I didn't wait until people were looking and making a scene. I just did what I knew God would have me do with a great attitude. In just a couple of months, corporate came to me and asked if I would like a salary position making three times what I was making. Many times people would happen to see my dedication to truth and say, "Why are you doing more than you're getting paid for?" They didn't understand I wasn't doing it for the company but I was doing it for my father in heaven.

Jesus never said we wouldn't have trials, but he did say to count it all joy when going through trials and tribulations (James 1:2). The kingdom of God is the upside-down kingdom. God requires we live our lives according to the Word of God, and the world lives their lives according to the world's knowledge. This is why it is so important that we read and apply God's Word daily because it washes wrong thinking out and helps us to think like God (Ephesians 5:26). We can't know God's purpose if we don't first know his Word. The Bible states that God's people perish spiritually because they don't take the time to know his Word (Hosea 4:6). Seek first the kingdom in all you do, say, and think, and God will do the rest (Matthew 6:33). We should never allow our plan to rob us of God's purpose. Kim and I love you. Have a super awesome day.

The Gift

Have you ever received a gift that wasn't wrapped? Maybe you've given a gift that wasn't wrapped. Would you rather receive a gift that isn't wrapped or a gift that is meticulously wrapped with beautiful paper and a ribbon with awesome curls? A wrapped gift builds anticipation. It's exciting to peel the paper and discover the thoughtfulness of the giver.

Our lives are the same way. Sometimes it's not just about our gifting that God has given us, but rather how we present and give that gift that matters. God has blessed each and every one of us with a gift or ability that we are good at. What makes that gift special and appealing is being wrapped in the love of God and adorned with God's truth. For example, I have a gift to communicate. If I just say whatever I want rather than being led by the spirit of God, then I'm not helping overcome anything. Instead I run the risk of causing hurt and increasing the problem. When we take our gift and allow God's covering to guide us, we can be most effective in helping others solve their problems. We can also help people find joy, happiness, and peace when offering Jesus through our beautiful gifting.

The Bible is our standard. When we allow the truth of God to transform us into what God has for our lives, then everyone around us can see the beautiful gift that God has made us to be. This is how we fulfill our purpose in Christ. God's Word is absolute truth. When we apply God's truth, it gives birth to love, and love conquers all (1 Corinthians 13). God has literally empowered us with the answer to everything: his love! So as you start your day, seek truth through God's Word. Allow his love to be the wrapping paper of your gifting. Know that in God, there is nothing we can't accomplish (Philippians 4:13). So go and give your gift using your abilities to make a difference in the lives around you. Kim and I love you. Have a great day!

Who Are We?

I was reading in the book of Mark, chapter 5, yesterday, and Jesus was dealing with a man possessed by demons. Everyone who had dealt with this man in the past couldn't even keep him bound. This man had supernatural strength and was constantly breaking his chains and restraints. Today Hollywood has made demon possession something that only a few can overcome, and even then its a battle sometimes not ending well for the priest or person doing the exorcism.

When we read the account in Mark, it's a totally different situation. Not only did Jesus cast the devils out, but when the demons saw Jesus, they begged not to be cast out of the region. The demons asked if Jesus had come to imprison them before their time. Notice Jesus didn't need holy water, he didn't have to argue with the demons, and he didn't have to stomp his feet and chant. Jesus simply told them to leave, and the man's mind was made whole.

If Jesus is in us and we are the righteousness of God in Christ, then why aren't we casting out devils and setting the captives free? The problem is we as the church don't know who we are and the power we posses. Why? Because we aren't reading our Bibles! When we read and apply the Word of God in our lives, we become more and more of a reflection of who Jesus is. The power that was made available to us is evident when dealing with healing the sick, casting out devils, raising the dead, or just the everyday trials we face in life. The more we read, the more we know and the more confident we become in all that Jesus said we can do. Jesus made a profound statement; he said, "The things I do, you will do and even greater" (John 14:12). God has amazing plans for each and every one of our lives (Jeremiah 29:11), so read your Bibles and walk in all that God has for your life. Kim and I love you and are excited to see what all God has for you.

Whose Image Are You a Reflection Of?

Christianity is a journey, a refining process. When we first ask Jesus into our hearts, we at best can say we are a good person. But the reality is this, we are human! We lie, cheat, steal, gossip, are sexually immoral, are stingy, and the list goes on. Now I realize that these are extremes, and in today's day and age, these aren't even considered sin; they are referred to as life choices. The reason Satan wants to confuse or blur the line of what is or isn't sin is because if he can get us to buy into the way of thinking that sin is just a life choice, then there is no need for a Savior. Then the importance of what Jesus did on the cross is of no value.

The reality is, without Jesus in our hearts, we are a lost and dying generation that doesn't even know that there is a problem. When we ask Jesus into our lives and we begin to read and apply the Word of God to our lives, we begin to see just how much we need God. As we look into the Word of God, it reveals the true reflection of who we really are (James 1:23).

The Bible states that we were created in the image of who God is (Genesis 1:27). So who is God? God is love (1 John 4:7-21). He sees our potential for greatness and not our problems. He keeps no records of wrongs (1 Corinthians 13:5). The amazing thing about sin is people don't go to hell because they are sinners but they go to hell because they deny the answer to sin. If I am drowning, the water has the potential to kill me, but what really kills me is my unwillingness to get into the lifeboat.

Yes sin is a problem but the real problem is we deny what Jesus accomplished on the cross. As a result, we allow sin to separate us from God's best, and eventually we die and go to hell (Isaiah 59:2). When we get saved, Jesus comes into our heart, and through his Word, we begin to see the true reflection of all that God is and has for our lives. The more we conform to his Word, the more we begin to look like him (Romans 12:2). People are able to experience him in all his glory because we are now that lifeboat for others. The Bible refers to our lives as good fruit (Matthew 7:17). Good fruit is juicy and tastes amazing. Good fruit provides nutrition to the person who is eating it and is a source of life.

People should see Jesus in all that we do, say, and think. That doesn't mean that we should go around beating people up with the Word of God thinking we are better than others. We should be a source of peace, joy, and love. When the question is asked what is different about our lives, we should have enough of the Word inside us to lead people to the saving grace of Jesus Christ. Our lives should be 95 percent what people see and, when needed, 5 percent what we can tell them. People are led by example. So as we start our day, let's seek Jesus, allowing our lives to be a true reflection of God's amazing faithfulness, and bring hope to a world that is hopeless. Kim and I love you and are excited for all that God is doing in you through you and for you. Have a great day.

A True Reflection

Jesus is the light of this world (John 8:12). We are instructed in the Word of God not to hide our light but rather to let it shine (Matthew 5:15). If Jesus is the light and the light lives in our hearts, then our lives should be an illumination of Jesus and the light that he provides. After all, out of our heart flow the issues of life (Proverbs 4:23). When we look in the mirror, we see a crisp, clear reflection of what we look like to others. Jesus was and is the exact representation of who the father is (John 14:9). Jesus stated several times through the Word that if you have seen him, you have seen the Father, because the Father and he are one. This is an example to us as to what we should be to others. We should be able to say, "If you have seen me, you have seen Jesus, because Jesus and I are one." In 2 Timothy 3:1-7, it states that in the last days, men will be self-centered and all about themselves. We see this all around us everywhere we look. The good news is that God has called us to live and be a reflection of the goodness of God in the greatest time the world has ever known: the time of Christ's return.

When we look at Jesus and the life he lived on this earth, his entire life was all about serving and loving people. The Bible states that it's the love of God through us that draws all men to know and understand salvation and everything Christ accomplished on the cross for us (Romans 2:4). When we understand who we are in Christ, then we are able to let go of seeking our own wants and desires and our own needs because we understand that all who we are and all that we need has been provided in the accomplishments of the cross. We can cast our cares on him because he cares for us (1 Peter 5:7). We can rest in knowing that our needs are met according to his riches and glory (Philippians 4:19). We can be confident in where life takes us because our footsteps are divinely ordered (Psalms 37:23). We can have peace in the midst of a life storm because all things, good or bad, work together for our good because we love God and are called according to his purpose (Romans 8:28). These are just a few of the things that define us as a Christians and empowers us to get our eyes off us and wholly on what God desires to do in us, through us, and for us as we reach the lost and dying while displaying God's love to them. As a result of our stability in Christ, we can be consistent in what we are doing because God is our strength (Psalms 28:7). The reason that God has provided everything needed in every aspect of life is so that we can be consistent and focus on what allows us to be fruitful in his kingdom.

The Word instructs us to seek first the kingdom in all that we say, think, and do, and everything else will be added unto us (Matthew 6:33). We as a nation have defined ourselves by what we have the size of our homes, the luxury of our cars, boats, and such, and our social status of keeping up with the Joneses. Luke 12:15 states for be on our guard against all sorts of greed, as a man does not consist in the abundance of his possessions. We are just stewards. We will never truly own anything. When we stand before God, he will ask what we did with what we were given. His provision is to fulfill the vision or purpose that God has for your ministry in this world. Proverbs 28:25 states a greedy man stirs up dissention, but he who trusts in the Lord will prosper. We have become the righteousness of God in Christ set apart and made whole by the blood of the lamb for the sole purpose of loving people and loving God while fulfilling our purpose in this earth (2 Corinthians 5:21). Kim and I love you and are super excited as we work together to allow many to come to know and understand the fullness of God's love. Have a great day.

When Bad Things Happen

I was thinking about my accident and how it has tested my faith. The aftermath of the accident not only tests our faith but reveals our character of who we are in Christ. The enemy is quick to whisper all sorts of uncertainties. Satan uses every tactic to keep us from standing on and relying in our Savior and all the promises that God's Word offers. When the storm comes, the wind is blowing, hail surrounds us, and we are beaten by torrential rains, this is the time we need to run to God and stand on his Word (Matthew 7:24).

When I get up in the morning and my legs won't work, I speak God's promises. Thank you, God, that your promises are "yes" and "amen" (2 Corinthians 1:20) and that my footsteps are divinely ordered (Psalms 37:23). When the devil says you are going to lose your job and asks what you are going to do about the house note that is eleven days late, you speak the Word! Thank you, God, that you are my provider (Philippians 4:19), that you make a way when there is no way (Philippians 2:13), and you give me favor with people (Proverbs 3:4). I thank you that your Word is faithful, true, and just. Thank you that your mercies are new every morning (Lamentations 3:22-24).

When we stay strong and apply God's Word to our problems, that's when the miracle takes place. I can't imagine having to go through this and not having God's Word and all his promises to trust in. When we stand on God's Word, maintaining a good attitude, while using our situation to advance the gospel by loving people, then we experience true power and all that God has for our lives. I encourage you, if you are going through a problem, draw near to God by reading and applying his Word. The Bible states that God searches throughout the earth looking for a faithful heart that he can bless (2 Chronicles 16:9). Kim and I love you and want greatness for your lives! Have a super awesome day!

Why, God, Why?

Give all of yourself to a trusting God! There are times when we don't understand why things happen. We want to know why prayers aren't answered. Why do bad things happen? We don't have to always understand in order to trust. God gives us his Word to encourage us, to inform us, to build our faith, and to give us the ability to trust (2 Timothy 3:16). We should strive to get to a point in our lives where no matter what the devil throws at us or what he shows us, we can rest easy in knowing God is in control (1 Peter 5:7). When we trust God, then all situations will work out to his glory and our benefit.

I went to the doctor today to have some test run. The enemy was quick to imply that it could be this or that. Then he asked, "What are you going to do?" Fear began to rise up and play on the what-ifs. As a Christian, I either trust God or I don't. I began to inform Satan that he is a liar and the truth is not in him (John 8:44). God has not given me a spirit of fear (2 Timothy 1:7). God will finish what he started in me, and instantly the fear went away (Philippians 1:6)!

God is in control, and regardless of the situation, we need to trust God. He is for us, and no weapon formed against us will prosper (Romans 8:31, Isaiah 54:17). Total trust in God and the power of his Word and all that was purchased through the blood of Jesus will lead us in a life of victory. Kim and I love you. Have a great day!

Wisdom and Understanding

God's Word is amazing. It has the answers for all life's problems and gives us the total favor of God, denying us nothing. So if this is the case and we know it's true because God is not a man that he should lie and his Word is true, faithful, and just (Numbers 23:19), then why don't we read and apply what we know to be so true?

Someone once said, "Stupid is as stupid does." God's Word states that the same wisdom and understanding that created the world is available to us. When applied, it yields us God's favor, brings healing, gives us sweet sleep, allows for wealth and prosperity, and makes a way where there is no way. God's Word gives us unlimited favor and peace while the rest of the world is crumbling from the pressures of life. The list of benefits goes on and on.

In God, we live, move, and have our being (Acts 17:28). Giving our lives fully to seeking wisdom and under- standing allows God to give all that he has promised while helping us soar like eagles. Rise above, and live the blessed life. The Bible states, "Let a man not be fooled in his heart. Whatever he sows, that shall he reap" (Galatians 6:7). If we seek God, giving all that we are in living a life of wisdom and understanding, there is nothing God won't do for us. Wow! God is so amazing (Ephesians 3:20). He has great things for us and wants only the best. My challenge for today is to read Proverbs chapters 1-3 and experience God's plan for success. Kim and I love you, believe in you, and know that God has great things for you. Have a super awesome day.

You Can Only Pretend So Long _____

I have mentored many people in the faith over the years. I have seen some grow and become all that God desires for their lives. The Word of God enables us to literally do the impossible. We all want the benefits that God offers through his Word. When the storms come and oppositions strike, we often retreat to what is most comfortable.

The Israelites are a great example of this very thing. God had amazing plans for the people of Israel. God not only wanted them to be delivered out of Egypt's bondage but also wanted to give them the more than enough blessing. Giving them the Promised Land of milk and honey! The problem is Israel wanted the promises of God in their lives, but every time opposition struck, they wanted to go back to Egypt, their familiar place. Egypt was anything but ideal. The people were overworked and treated badly, even killed. Despite Egypt's harsh environment, the people's basic needs were met. God's desire is that we all have and experience the fullness of all that is made available in God's Word through the death, burial, and resurrection of his son Jesus. The truth is we can't experience greatness if we don't do the impossible. We can only accomplish the impossible when we are willing to read and apply God's Word to our lives.

Many times I have seen my protégés talk the talk but produce no fruit in their lives. We can't fake fruit. Faithfulness in God produces life-giving fruit. Fruit is for the sole purpose of giving nourishment to those who eat it. If our fruit isn't bringing life to the lost and dying, then we aren't fulfilling our true purpose.

We can only fake faith for so long. Eventually the proof will be in the pudding. True fruit is a manifestation of God's promises and his faithfulness for our lives. A wax apple might appear to look juicy and delicious, but if we were to bite into a wax apple, we would not have a great experience. We would never forget the experience of that wax apple. True, fruit not only has a lasting memory but brings nourishment that produces health in our lives.

The Simplicity of a Practical Jesus

We should always be quick to apply God's Word, allowing him to empower us for greatness and the beauty of bearing good fruit. Kim and I love you. Have a great day.

Do You Have a Parachute?

What is the difference between believing and having faith? Faith is having a parachute, and believing is having an idea of a parachute. Faith gets the job done, and believing brings failure and disappointment. Faiths says, "I have a key to this car, and if I put it in the igni- tion and turn it. the car will start, and I can drive wherever I want." Believing says the same thing but has no key! The Bible says that true faith comes from the Word of God (Romans 10:17). The more of the Word we have, the stronger our faith. Believing that God will do whatever we need in our lives but never having his Word in our lives only leads to despair. The disappointment of never receiving what we are believing for, stating this just doesn't work. The only reason it didn't work is because it wasn't empowered by the application of God's Word!

Here is the long and the short. God has amazing things that he wants to do in our lives, and he has plans for us that would blow our minds. The reality is, if we are not a student of God's Word, then we will never experience any of what he has for us. Someone asked me why is it that every day the whole of the message is, "Read your Bible"? Because it's the foundation for everything that God wants to do in our lives. There can be nothing without God's Word in our lives on a daily basis. Just hope deferred, and that makes the heart sick! If we want to change the world and experience the fullness of all that God has for us, then we need to be a student of his Word! Kim and I love you and are excited for the plans and purpose that God has for your life! Have a great day.

Allowing Pain to Become Your Strength

Life is full of disappointments, and many times in life people hurt us, take advantage of us, and despitefully use us. Someone once stated that we can be pitiful or powerful, but we can't be both. For years I carried my past around, never really getting past the multitude of wrongs done to me by people who were supposed to love me. I allowed my worth and future to be dictated by my past. We can never effectively go forward if we are constantly looking backward (Luke 9:62).

Although I loved God and was saved, I didn't know how to let go and be the victor that God's Word said I could be. I began to read and apply the Word of God to my life, and I understood that I am more than a conqueror (Romans 8:37). I wasn't a victim but a victor. Although people had said I was unworthy of love and that no one could love me, Jesus loved me. The Father sees me as the apple of his eye. Once I began renewing my mind, it freed me to receive healing in my life.

When we don't have a plan for our future, then our future is threatened to be a repeat of our past. The Word of God was the plan for my future, and it stopped the cycle of that victim mentality and set me free bringing the healing I needed to accomplish God's plan and purpose for my life. I'm not saying that I don't experience disappointment from time to time or that people don't still hurt my feelings.

The Bible states to count it all joy in trials and tribulations (James 1:2). Why? Because when we trust God, then every disappointment becomes an opportunity for us to walk in victory and even bring healing to those who use and hurt us. The fact is hurting people hurt people. When we allow God's love to flow through us, it allows God to work in our abusers' lives, drawing them to a place of understanding. This allows them to receive healing and experience their destiny in Christ while fulfilling their purpose in this earth. The same healing and freedom that Jesus so freely blessed me with, I can now give   to someone else.

A couple years ago, Kim and I were involved in a large church. We volunteered 3-4 times a week, we loved as many people as we could, and we actively discipled people. Our heart was to help them to know and understand all that was available to them in and through God's Word. One of these people was a practicing witch, and she called the church and said that Kim and I came to her house, robbed her, and stole her car, and that she was afraid for her life. The following Sunday we came to church only to be met by the pastor and the police. They escorted Kim and I off the premises and said that if we ever came back, we would be arrested. Wow! This was definitely a blow to Kim's and my faith. But as we know, all things, good or bad, work together for our good because we love God and are called according to his purpose (Romans 8:28). Kim and I still pray for this lady's soul, because without Jesus, hell is her only destination.

The Word of God takes what Satan means for harm and literally empowers us to be a lifeline for the lost and dying. The truth is this: it isn't about me or you but it's about Jesus in me or you. The only way we can go from a pitiful victim to a powerful victor is to see opposition through the power of God's Word. Satan has a plan, but when we trust God, Satan's plan is replaced with God's purpose. Kim and I love you and are excited for you to enjoy the freedom of an overcoming lifestyle. Have a great day.

Purpose versus Destiny

What is our destiny? When we don't have Jesus in our lives, we literally have no destiny (2 Peter 3:9). When we make Jesus Lord over our lives, we fulfill our destiny. What is the next step? How do we fulfill purpose in our lives?

A life without purpose is like having a new Ferrari and no gas! It looks great but can't take us anywhere. Our lives can never be made complete if we don't fulfill our purpose in Christ Jesus! God's purpose for our lives is that we experience the manifestation of all his promises in our lives while using our God- given gifts and talents to reach this lost and dying world. We use our gifts and abilities in every day life for all sorts of things. Our gifts and abilities are only brought to the fullness of God's potential when we allow the love of God to flow through our gifts and abilities, affecting the lives around us.

The last thing Jesus commanded us was to go into all the world and make disciples of others (Mark 16:15). So how does God's love through us accomplish that? Well, first we need to know and understand the tools that are available to us by reading and applying God's Word. His Word is absolute. It teaches us how to be free from the stress and anxieties of this world (1 Peter 5:7). God's Word sculpts us into the exact representation of who Jesus is. Our lives become lifelines to the lost and dying, allowing God's love to lead people to a place of restoration. Now they too can fulfill their destiny in Christ and understand their purpose! So many times our lives are nothing more than a display of a victim mentality, powerless to change not only our lives but the lives of others.

Today is a new day and a new beginning. God's Word is true, faithful, and just (Proverbs 30:5). His promises are "yes" and "amen" (2 Corinthians 1:20). God has literally empowered us for greatness. So let us rise up, shake off the victim mentality, seek God in his Word, and display mightily our victory. The only thing God needs is a willing heart, and he will do the rest. Wow! Kim and I love you and are excited for you to experience your destiny in Christ while fulfilling your purpose in this earth.

Darkness Is Nothing More Than the Absence of Light

We do not have to live a life in the dark. When I am at home, if I walk into a room and it is dark, I don't complain about the darkness. I just flip a switch, and the light comes on. When the light comes on, the darkness goes away. Light and dark cannot occupy the same space. When we live our lives without Jesus, we choose to live a life full of darkness. Oftentimes the darkness breeds despair, loneliness, depression, hopelessness, and every other negative tactic Satan uses to convince us there is no light switch. Always remember Satan is the father of all lies and knows no truth (John 8:44). The only power he has is the power of suggestion (Genesis 3, Matthew 4:6). We can either choose to believe a lie or seek truth.

I am amazed at how many people choose to live a life of darkness while believing a liar who knows no truth. Jesus is the light of the world, and when we have Christ in our lives, his light removes the darkness from us (John 8:12). In him there is joy, and where there is joy, there is no despair. Jesus gives us hope, and where there is hope, there is no hopelessness. Jesus is like a friend that sticks with us closer than a brother (Proverbs 18:24). In Jesus, there is no loneliness. God gives us a sound mind, so in him, there is no depression (2 Timothy 1:7). The more we seek God in reading and applying his Word, the more truth we have. Truth always set us free from the darkness (Luke 4:18).

The choice is ours. We can either live in despair and darkness or simply flip the switch and allow Jesus to be the light in our world. In Christ, we are literally empowered to accomplish anything because he is our strength. Or we can stay in the dark with no hope of a better tomorrow. The cool thing about allowing the light of Jesus to shine in our lives is it draws others out of the darkness and into his marvelous light. The more people you allow to experience the light, the brighter Jesus shines. If I have one flashlight and then two, three, and so on, the next thing you know, we make a spotlight that reaches farther and burns brighter. If your life is dark and hopeless, Kim and I encourage you to ask Jesus into your heart and begin reading and applying God's Word to your life. Allow your life to become a lighthouse that pierces the darkness, leading others to experience God's love, mercy, grace, and compassion, bringing hope of a brighter tomorrow. Kim and I love you and pray for you daily. Have a great day.

Created to Lead, Not Follow

The Bible states, "Be not conformed to this world, but be transformed by the renewing of your mind through the washing of the Word" (Romans 12:2). The word *conform* according to the *Webster* dictionary states that to conform is "to obey or agree with something, to behave in a way that is acceptable by most people."

Why do you think that God doesn't want us to conform to the majority? Because the last thing Jesus said was to go into all the world and make disciples of all (Mark 16:15). We were created to lead, not follow! The word *transformed* means "to change something completely and usually in a good way, to change the outward appearance, or to change in character or condition." As we begin to read and apply the Word of God, it first trains our brain to think like God. When we put the Word in our heart, it allows our lives to be transformed into the perfect reflection of who Jesus is. An inward change always results in an outward change. The word *renew* means "to make like new: restore to freshness, vigor or perfection." When Adam allowed sin into his life through a wrong way of thinking, it gave birth to the destruction or consequences of sin. When we read the Word, God instructs us how to be restored to the perfection that he had intended for us from the very beginning.

The other day I was watching a movie on regular TV. During the course of the movie, I saw the same commercial twenty times! Why do they need to play the same thing twenty times in four hours? It's called programming. So I looked up *programming* and the definition of *brainwashing. Webster* says that *brainwashing* is "a forcible indoctrination to induce someone to give up basic political, social, or religious beliefs and attitudes and to except contrasting regimented ideas by persuasion, propaganda, or salesmanship." Television, radio, magazines, and billboards are all forms of programming. Why is it called programming, and who do they hope to program?

Have you ever watched the news and they are expecting a storm? They always talk about the what-ifs or the potential for destruction.

201

When it isn't as bad as first reported, they switch gears and talk about how devastating in could have been. Why? To instill fear. One of the key factors to controlling someone is instilling fear. The Word of God states that he has not given us a spirit of fear but of sound mind, good judgment, and the ability to love (2 Timothy 1:7). God knew we would be bombarded with fear of the unknown, yet over 365 times in his Word he states to fear not. It is vitally important that we read and apply the Word in our lives.

Our lives are a reflection of how we think. Either we are programmed with things that are contrary to the Word of God or we learn to think like God. Through God's Word, we are empowered to accomplish the impossible while leading many to come to know and understand the saving grace of Jesus Christ! You can't lead others to freedom through truth if you don't first know truth yourself! I'm not saying TV, radio, and such are wrong, but I will say that it's definitely wrong programming. Think about this: TV and radio are transmitted through the air. Satan is the prince of the air. That doesn't mean all programming is wrong. It just means Satan has a plan and purpose for our lives. Don't allow yourself to be manipulated. Allow God's Word to lead you in truth for your life. After all, as a man thinks, so is he (Proverbs 23:7). Where the mind goes, the man follows. Have a great day. Kim and I love you and are cheering you on!

We Are All Created for a Purpose

When we walk in the fullness of God's Word, we are fulfilling our destiny while walking in the purpose that God has for our lives. The last thing Jesus said as he ascended into heaven was go into all the world and make disciples of all men (Mark 16:15). The Bible states that the love of God through us draws all men to an understanding of who Jesus is and all that was made available to us on the cross (Romans 2:4). Salvation is not our purpose but rather our destiny in Christ. Our purpose is when we allow God's Word to transform our lives while using our gifts and talents to accomplish God's plans for our lives. We can't disciple anyone in truth until we first know truth ourselves.

What is truth? The Word of God is absolute truth (John 17:17). God instructs us that we should not put our faith or trust in any man but rather every word that proceeds out of his mouth (Psalms 146:3, Matthew 4:4). Why? Because God is not a man that he should lie (Numbers 23:19). When we walk out of our lives reflecting God's goodness and his mercy, we are not only qualified to share truth, but our lives are a reflection of truth. Why is this so important?

We are literally putting our money where our mouth is. We are a walking testimony of all that God's Word says is available in us, through us, and for us. Knowledge is power. The more we know, the more power that is available to us, the clearer the reflection of who God is in our lives. It's no longer by our might but by his might (2 Corinthians 12:9). Doors are opened, lives are changed, and truth is realized. You can be pitiful or powerful, defeated or an overcomer. Our level of success depends on our will- ingness to seek out God's truth in his Word for our lives. When we fail, it's because we choose to fail. We can change the world when we choose to walk in all that God has for us. Rise up, fulfill your destiny, and walk in the purpose that defines all that God is. Kim and I love you and pray that you find and fulfill your purpose in Christ. Have a great day.

Copycat

Satan is the biggest copycat the world will ever experience. Satan's whole desire is to be like God (Isaiah 14:14). So if God is truth and the opposite of truth is a lie, then Satan is a liar. In fact, God states in his Word that Satan is the father of lies and he knows no truth (John 8:44). Satan's greatest weapon is the power of suggestion (Genesis 3:1, Matthew 4:6). Satan hopes that we will believe his suggestion, therefore robbing us of our identity in Christ Jesus.

According to God's Word, we are the righteousness of God in Christ set apart and made whole by the blood of the Lamb (1 Peter 1:2, 1 Corinthians 6:11). If Satan can keep us from understanding who we are in Christ, then he knows in and of ourselves we can do nothing, rendering us powerless. I have two examples of this in the Word. First was Eve. Eve was already like God. She was immortal, and she had everything needed and/or wanted to live a great life. God fellowshipped with her daily, and there was no sickness. Eve's life was made perfect in God. Satan's lie was this: "God doesn't want you to eat of the tree because God knows that when you do, you will be like him." Eve was already like God, made in his image. But because she believed a liar, she lost all that God had given her. The second example would be Jesus when he was in the wilderness. Satan said, "If you are the son of God, why?" Because Satan knew that if he could get Jesus to believe his lie, then he could keep Jesus from fulfilling all that the Father had for Jesus in redeeming humanity on the cross.

So when Satan suggests that God is mad at us because of some- thing we did or didn't do (Lamentations 3:22), we need to realize that God's mercies are new every morning and his forgiveness is seventy times seven daily (Matthew 18:22). God is not mad at us; he is mad about us! When Satan tries to get us to buy into guilt and condemnation, we need to realize that in Christ, there is no condemnation or guilt (Romans 8:1). These are just a couple of ways Satan tries to steal our identity. That's why we need to read our

Bible—so that we know who we are in Christ and all that Jesus accomplished for us (2 Timothy 2:15). Then when Satan comes with his lies, he can't steal our identity in Christ. In Christ, you can do all things (Philippians 4:13). So we need to read our Bible to learn who God says we are. We need to educate ourselves on the lies and schemes of the enemy, never again allowing him to steal our identity and render- ing us powerless. Kim and I love you and are excited for all that God has for you. Have a great day!

Communication

It's two thirty in the a.m., and I was thinking about the importance of good communication. Many times we say one thing but the other person hears something totally different. Sometimes we communicate, but it's not done properly. A perfect example of this is, if I have a bank account and I walk in to the bank and say, "Give me some money," they may hear, "Give me your money, I'm robbing you," If you say, "Hello, my name is Kirk, my account number is such, and I need to make a withdrawal," then they will do what they need to do in order to fulfill my request. One way may land us in jail, and the other fulfills our need.

God is the same way. Have you ever heard someone pray and they said, "If it's your will"? That is not a prayer of faith. The Bible says that when we pray, we should pray according to God's will, and when we do so, God will not only hear our prayers but will answer them (1 John 5:14). The Bible states that faith comes from hearing the Word (Romans 10:17) and a man without faith is unpleasing to God (Hebrews 11:6). So as you begin to hide the Word of God in your hearts through reading and applying his Word, your hearts are filled with faith.

God then instructed us according to the Word on how to pray. For example, someone might have cancer and pray, "If it's your will, then heal me." The Bible states that Jesus took thirty-nine lashes on his back so we can have and experience provision for healing (Isaiah 53:5). Here is an example of an effective prayer:

> "Father, thank you for all that Jesus accomplished on the cross, and I thank you that because of the lashes he took on his back, I am healed. In Jesus's name, amen."

This is a prayer of faith because it is God's will. God also states that when we pray according to the Word, he watches over his Word to perform it (Jeremiah 1:12). God's Word will never return void (Isaiah 55:11). God's Word will accomplish all that it was sent to do. The

The Simplicity of a Practical Jesus

Bible says the power of life and death is in the tongue (Proverbs 18:21). Jesus said he is the way, the truth, and the life (John 14:6). Jesus is the word made flesh (John 1:14). When we speak God's Word, we are literally speaking life. The Bible states, "Let a man not be fooled in his heart. Whatever he sows, that will he reap" (Galatians 6:7). So speak life and reap all that God has for your life.

If you're not sure what God's will is concerning your situation, get into your Bible and learn how to prosper in every area of your life. Learn to speak life into every area of your life (Romans 4:17). God loves you and has unlimited possibilities for your life. Have a great day, and always remember Kim and I love you and are cheering for you!

Choose Life

As I sat and was scrolling through my social network, I wept as I learned of my friend's untimely death. Not so much because we were close, so to speak, but rather because of his need for a Savior. Many of you know I had a body shop years ago, and this man had an upholstery shop across the street from me. We didn't talk much as I was looked at as a joke to him and his friends. They all had cool hot rods, custom Harleys, and were very popular with any and all who were in the so-called cool crowd. I remember this man coming by the shop one day and the opportunity I had to share Jesus with him. As I gave him truth of our need for a Savior, he just said, "I don't believe in any of that." He also made the statement, "When you're dead, you're dead," and walked away. I remember weeping that day because I was sad that he was so sure that Jesus wasn't something he needed.

The truth of the matter is, no man can enter heaven without a Savior. There are so many people in our everyday lives that are lost and dying and will split hell wide open not because they are wicked or even bad people but because they don't have Jesus in their lives. We need to live our lives as an examples of truth, reflecting Jesus in our lives for all to see. My heart is so sad because I know that if he could come back for just a moment's time, he would say, "I was wrong. Turn my heart to Jesus." It is so important that we read our Bibles so that our lives are a beautiful reflection of God's love, mercy, and compassion, bringing hope to the lost and dying. My hope is that God's mercy was there as he lay in that hospital bed, and in his last few minutes, he chose to ask Jesus into his heart. Much love and many blessings to the friends and family members of this great loss. Kim and I love you and will continue to keep you in our thoughts and prayers.

Believing Is Not a Relationship

In John, chapter 3, one of the religious leaders came to Jesus and acknowledged that he knew that Jesus was sent by God. Jesus told him, "Unless you experience relationship with the creator, you will never get the big picture." The Bible states that Satan believes in God and trembles in his presence (James 2:19). Many times in life we might believe the validity of God's Word and all that has been accomplished on the cross, but unless we understand by applying it to our lives, then we are no different than those who believe and don't know the truth.

This is the difference between having faith in what is true and just believing. Faith comes from hearing the Word or bending our knee to the authority of God's Word (Romans 10:17). Faith in the Word of God brings results and gives us the ability to reflect God's faithfulness in our lives. When Kim and I got saved, we cut ties with all our friends that were a part of our other life BC—life before Jesus. We felt that this was what God was instructing us to do. The Bible states that bad company corrupts good morals (1 Corinthians 15:33).

So the other day I called one of our old friends, and the result was awful. They cussed me out and ranted that they had seen Kim and I on Facebook being all kissy kissy, and it made them sick. They said that I was deceived and would someday wake up and realize how deceived I was. They went on to accuse me of being a religious bigot and told me that they hated me and God and that if he ever saw me, he would shoot me. Wow.

The book of John states that evildoers hate the light because it exposes their evil. Evil flourishes in darkness, and Jesus is the light of the world, and when he lives in us and through us, his light pierces the darkness and exposes evil. John declared that as he heard the voice of Jesus, he was complete. John went on to say that Jesus has to become greater and we have to become less if we are to be effective in reaching the lost and dying. People don't care about our opinions, and when they stand before God on judgment day, God isn't going to ask them what my opinion was; he is going to ask what my word said.

As we begin to seek God out in our lives by reading and applying the Word of God to our lives (Romans 12:2), it literally transforms us into the perfect reflection of all that Jesus is and our imperfections begin to fade away. God has an amazing plan and purpose for your life, and as you seek him and cultivate your rela- tionship with him daily, you are literally empowered to accomplish the impossible. The Bible states that God will use the foolish things in this world to confound the wise (1 Corinthians 1:27). In and of ourselves, we are foolish and without power, but through Christ we can do all things. Kim and I love you. Have a great day.

A Great Paradigm Shift

I have been watching different posts on social media of people's ideas and intentions on many subjects. These subjects range from the voting candidates, gun rights, veterans, gay and lesbian agendas, transgender rights, the legalization of marijuana, the national anthem at sporting events, the embrace of Muslim rights, and the decline of Christianity. These issues are not just in our country but around the world. A paradigm shift is when we as a whole go from one way of thinking to a new way of thinking. This shift in thinking brings about many changes in many of the issues that I listed above.

The Bible states that as a man thinks in his heart, so is he (Proverbs 23:7). The Bible states that as it was in the days of Noah, so shall it be in the coming of Christ (Matthew 24:37). For years we as the church have been trying to get unbelievers to understand that Jesus is coming. The other day I was listening to an interview with one of the world's number one rappers, and he stated that soon Christ will return and the Christians or the problems will be removed and the world will finally be free to do as they want. As a country, we were founded on many truths that made us who we are, but those standards and truths are being removed and the pride of a people that say we don't need God and that we can do it on our own will soon understand the truth of the saying "Pride comes before the fall" (Proverbs 16:18).

We often post our disgust of this or that, and we have good intentions, but the reality is we are the minority. The time is fast approaching for the return of our Lord and Savior Jesus Christ, and one day soon every knee will bow and every tongue will confess Jesus is Lord (Romans 14:11). As we see the decline of humanity and the pure disgust of the masses regarding Christianity, draw close to the Word of God and take daily inventory of your lives, for our redemp- tion draws near (Luke 21:28).

Continue to love people and have a heart after God. God is the same yesterday, today, and forevermore (Hebrews 13:8). How do I know that the rapture will come before the tribulation? That is how God has done it many times in the past. Before the flood, God removed his people (Genesis 6:9). Before he destroyed Sodom and Gomorrah, he removed his people (Genesis 19). Before the death angel passed through Egypt, God protected his people by the blood on the post (Exodus 12:23). The Bible states that Jesus's return will be like the flood. So we will be removed, and then destruction. Some say that it's not fair that if they don't serve God, then they're going to hell. In reality, if I was drowning in the ocean and someone threw me a lifeline, I wouldn't deny or resent their help.

The truth is, sin is the ocean, it's the problem, and Jesus is the Savior or the lifeline, and God is the provider of that lifeline. God is trying to save us from impending destruction. Call on the name of Jesus, for today is the day of salvation (Hebrews 3:15). Don't reply out of fear for the unknown but rather because the creator of all things loves you (John 3:16) and has an amazing plan and purpose for your life (Jeremiah 29:11). God loves you and is excited to have fellowship with you. God's not mad at you' he is mad about you. Kim and I love you and want God's best for you. Have a super awesome day.

A Plan versus Purpose

Satan has a plan, but Jesus has a purpose (John 10:10). The road to hell is paved with good intentions. A good intention is a plan with no purpose (Proverbs 14:12). The Bible says that Jesus came to give life abundantly. Satan just wants to steal, kill, and destroy every good thing that God has for our lives.

The good news is that even when Satan has a plan to destroy our lives, God promises to take Satan's plan and give it purpose for God's glory and our benefit (Romans 8:28). We can only achieve purpose in our lives through Jesus in our hearts (John 15:5). Anything less is just a good intention. Satan is always quick to point out our problems and accuse us (Revelation 12:9-11). Jesus never sees our problems but rather our potential (Colossians 1:22). Why?

When our purpose is in Christ, we have no other outcome but success. The Bible states that we can do all things because Christ is our strength (Philippians 4:13). God prospers everything we put our hands to do (Deuteronomy 28:8). Purpose is a sure way to experience success not only in this world but in heaven as well. Jesus told a story of people that would come to him on the Day of Judgment talking about their good intensions to help people. Jesus said, "Depart from me for I never knew you" (Matthew 7:23). Why? Because a plan with no purpose is nothing more than a good intention.

Stop and take a moment to evaluate your intentions. Make sure that you are empowered by God for the greater good of his kingdom. Don't just have a good plan to be a good person. Jesus stated that if you gain the world's success in every area of your life but lose your own soul, it's all for nothing (Matthew 16:26). Don't let Satan sell you a plan that will lead you nowhere. Allow God to give your life purpose, empowering you to change the world (Philippians 4:13). Kim and I love you. Have a great day.

A Shallow Christian versus a Deep Christian!

After Jesus was crucified, the disciples went back to fishing (John 21:3) because it's what they knew and it was comfortable, but God had called them to be fishers of men (Matthew 4:19). How many times has God called us to do something in our lives and we revert back to what we were doing because, well, it's easy and safe (Luke 9:62)?

Once Jesus was standing on the shoreline, the disciples had been fishing all night without catching a fish. Jesus called out to them and said to move their boat to deeper water and throw the nets over the right side of the boat, and they answered him saying, "We have been fishing all night and we are tired!" The significance is this: the disciples answered Jesus stating how they felt (tired). Have you ever not taken a task due to the way you feel? The difference between what we do as to what God ask us to do is this: although the disciples had been out all night, they had been working in their own strength and in the wrong spot. But then Jesus instructed them on where to fish and how to do it, and they caught so many fish their nets were tearing.

The greatest difference is your strength versus God's strength (Philippians 4:13). In and of ourselves, we can do nothing, but through Christ we can do all things. If we would take the time every day to read our Bibles and listen to God's instructions, we would't have to work so hard trying to accomplish life (Romans 12:2). The Bible says that our footsteps are divinely appointed and the Word of God is a lamp unto out feet (Psalms 37:23). The Bible states to seek God first in our lives, and he will work out the particulars (Matthew 6:33).

The difference between a shallow Christian and a deep Christian is simple: one tries to live life by their feelings and the other relies on God's instructions and his timing! One leaves you frustrated and the other gives you a sense of fulfillment. Also when we live life on our own, we are limited in what we can accomplish (Philippians 4:13), but when we rely on God, the sky is the limit as for what God will do in you through you and for you! Kim and I love you. Have a super awesome day!

Bible Thumper

Often when we hear the term *Bible thumper*, we think of all sorts of weird ways that people over the years have misrepresented the gospel. The other day I was referred to as one of these so-called thumpers. I had to stop and really take inventory of the way I have represented the gospel.

I am very passionate when it comes to the Word of God. The Word gives us certainty when this life offers no certainty (Psalms 147:11). The Word gives us peace when there are no alternates for true peace (Ephesians 2:13-18). The Word gives joy unspeakable over flowing and literally walks us through hardships with a smile.

Satan wants to steal your joy, kill your dreams, and destroy your relationship with your creator (John 10:10). God's Word and his faithfulness to his Word brings us through all adversity and always gives us hope (Jeremiah 1:12). God wants to be our everything. This is why he created us to enjoy the intimacy of a relationship with him (Ephesians 2:10)! He wants to share all that he is and has with us. His love for us is the purest most powerful life-changing experience anyone could ever have.

So if this is what it means to be a Bible thumper, then yes, I am. I can do all things through Christ, who is my strength (Philippians 4:13), because I choose to bask in the glory of an amazing relation with my creator. My goal in life is to love as many people as I can and lead twice as many to know God's faithfulness (Mark 16:15). I want them to know and experience God's love, mercy, grace, and compassion all wrapped up in a promise of salvation, making this intimate relationship with him eternal. Is it such a bad thing to want that for all the people I love and care about? It's true, you know. Just saying!

A Simple Plan

The beauty of living a life that honors God is the simplicity of how the blessings of God work in our lives (Isaiah 25:1). A lot of times we as people don't seek God's will for our lives but expect him to bless our lives (James 1:8). The Bible states that if we will seek first the kingdom of God in all we do, say, and think, then everything else will be added to us. Learn to life your life on purpose. What?

The whole point in reading your Bible is so we know how to apply God and all that he has for our lives. For example, do all things without grumbling and complaining (Philippians 2:14), but rather do all things with a grateful heart (1 Thessalonians 5:18)! Why? Because grumbling and complaining bring about a curse in our lives and allow the enemy to steal from us. A grateful heart gives us the ability to operate in a blessing allowing God to bring more blessings into our lives (Galatians 6:7). Another example, do your job as unto God. Why? Because when we do it unto him, it takes the pressures of being successful or prosperous in our endeavors off our shoulders and puts them on God. God is the one that prospers everything we put our hands to (Psalms 1:3). There are thousands of blessings that are available to us in the Bible, but every one of them depend on us to do our part and walk in obedience to the command attached to them (Deuteronomy 28:1-2). Cause and effect.

I do what God asks me to do, and he is faithful to do what he promises to do (Jeremiah 1:12). Don't hear what I'm not saying. I'm not saying that if I'm bad, God won't bless me. His promises were made available when Jesus died on the cross (John 19:28-30), but if I want to walk in the fullness of all that was made available to me, it requires me to do my part (James 1:8). Every time God asks you to do something in his Word, it's not to control you but it's to bless you! It's never for less; it's always for more (2 Chronicles 16:9). God's love and blessings are amazing, and to be honest, if we were to walk in the fullness of all that is available to us, we would never have to try and get people to follow Jesus, but rather they would be drawn to him because of the outward expression of who he is and all that he is doing in you, through you, and for you (John 12:32). God is amazing and wants nothing but great things for you.

Take the time every morning to put him first, read your Bible, and pray over your day and learn to live your life on purpose (Romans 12:2). Always pray and ask God to give you insight and understanding as you read your Bible, and as he reveals himself to you, apply what is revealed (Ephesians 5:26, James 1:5). If you get to a point where you are not hearing from God, then go back to the last thing that he asked you to do and make sure that you are applying it in your life. God will only continue to reveal his Word to you if you continue to apply all that he shows you (Luke 16:10). Kim and I love you and are excited for you to experience all that God has for you. Have a great day!

Choices

Our lives are a result of the choices we make. What choices are you making? The Bible states that God has set before us a blessing, a curse, life, and death. God then states chooses life (Deuteronomy 30:19). The Word of God empowers us to accomplish all things because Jesus is our strength (Philippians 4:13). God makes a way where there is no way. He prospers everything we put our hands to do (Deuteronomy 30:9). He has provided healing in every area of our lives because of what Jesus accomplished on the cross (Isaiah 53). His healing includes mental, emotional, physical, and spiritual wellness.

When Jesus willingly laid his life down for us, he provided a way for us to enjoy a restored relationship with him (2 Corinthians 5:18). God states that all things, good or bad, work together for our good because we love God and are called accord- ing to his purpose (Romans 8:28). God gives us favor with all the right people (Proverbs 3:4). He promises us that no weapon formed against him will prosper, and he gives us authority over all our adversaries (Isaiah 54:17, Ephesians 1:21). God states that we can put our faith and trust in every word that has come out of his mouth because he is not a man that he should lie (Numbers 23:19). God gives us the ability to take our thoughts captive and to walk in peace, hope, and love (2 Corinthians 10:5). God is not a respecter of persons; what he will do for me, he will do for you (Acts 10:34).

God will do all these things and so much more if we choose to follow Jesus. Choose to seek him in your life, to walk in love, and to read and apply his Word (Matthew 6:33). Choose this day whom you will serve (Joshua 24:15). Kim and I love you and want you to experience all God's promises for your life. We want to see you fulfill your purpose in this earth and allow God's love to shine in your lives, bringing health and wholeness to all that you come in contact with.

Are We Applying Ourselves?

Having the ability to do the impossible and actually doing the impossible are two totally different things (James 1:22). People have to have ability both first and foremost. The difference between the two is one acted on their ability and the other didn't. Imagine going to college and studying engineering. Some will skip class and not do their homework and fail. They have the same opportunities as the guy who has the 4.0 GPA but just never applied themselves. The second person comes to class but never studies and squeaks by with a low C. The final person comes and applies themselves 100 percent and graduates top of their class. Would it be unfair if the second person went to work for the same company but the 4.0 gets better pay and more perks? And who would you want building your highrise apartment, the guy who cared enough to apply himself or the guy who just did the bare minimum?

God has amazing plans for each and every one of our lives (Jeremiah 29:11). The same opportunities for greatness are available to any who will seek God's plan for their lives by applying his amazing Word to their lives (Acts 10:34). God is not a respecter of persons. God desires the very best for each and every one of us. Are you willing to step outside of the box and trust the faithfulness of God's love, mercy, grace, and compassion?

The Bible states that there are only two reasons people fail. First is due to a lack of knowledge of God's Word (Hosea 4:6, Proverbs 29:18); the second is a lack of vision for our lives. We can't have vision if we don't first know what all has been made available in God's Word through Jesus's sacrifice. We should seek God every morning and read and apply his Word to our lives (Romans 12:2, Lamentations 3:22-24). Allow God to empower you for the impossible while expe- riencing the fullness of his faithfulness. Kim and I love you. Have a super awesome day.

An "I Can't" Mentality

I have always been an upbeat, can-do kind of person and always willing to go the extra distance. When I had my body shop, the majority of my work came from other body shops that told the customer it couldn't be done!

As Christians, we should have the greatest outlook with nothing but optimism because we can do all things through Christ as our strength (Philippians 4:13). *I can't* only means two things. The first definition of *I can't* is "I don't know how." This is understandable. Many situations in life leave us stumped. The amazing thing about God's Word is it holds the answers for every issue life could ever throw our way (Proverbs 4:23). The only time it is okay to not know is when we stay in that category due to a lack or truth. The Bible states to study to show ourselves approved (2 Timothy 2:15).

This isn't for God's approval. When trials and tribulations or the storms of life come, we know how to not only weather the storm but how to overcome the storm (Matthew 7:24). The second explanation for *I can't* is we just don't want to. If God makes all things possible, then we have no excuse as to why we can't. I was building a 1977 full-size van, and I chopped the top eight inches. Not only was I told that it couldn't be done but I was told I couldn't suicide the doors either. Every one I talked to not only said it couldn't be done but was mad when I accomplished it.

The reason people will try and talk us out of doing the impossible is because if we succeed, then they don't have an excuse for not trying. If people can't keep us from doing the impossible, they will disapprove of our success. When I had to get the windshield cut for my van project, I called fifty glass companies. All fifty told me it couldn't be done. I got on the Internet and researched the art of cutting glass. I did what everyone told me was impossible. When I went to the nationals car show, my project not only took second place out of a thousand entries but I was the only one who had an original-cut glass. Many people came and asked who cut my glass. When we do the impossible through God's greatness, everyone wants to know where the answer came fRomans Because we do what others can't, we now are valuable in the eyes of those around us who have experienced the impossible through us.

The Bible states that many are called, but few are chosen (Matthew 22:14). Everyone is looking for answers but only seem to want the kind of answers that don't require effort. It's not God's desire that any man perish but that all should have eternal life (2 Peter 3:9). God calls all. Few are chosen! Why? Because only a few are willing to read and apply the truths of God's Word to their lives, accomplishing the impossible through God's faithfulness! Don't just ask Jesus into your heart so you can go to heaven but rather allow God's Word to transform your life, allowing you to do what others say can't be done (James 1:22). Kim and I love you. Have a great day.

A Perfect Plan

Why do we settle for less and even toxic relationships when God has the perfect solution to our loneliness? In 1999, I was lonely and wanted nothing more than to experience companionship. God had the very relationship I desired in mind (Psalms 37:23). If I would have headed the gentle tug at my heart, was patient, and trusted that God had my best interest at heart, I would have never had to endure the pain that left me broken, bleeding, and hopelessly lonelier than I was ten years prior.

I remember sitting under a tree reading my Bible and asking God for permission to marry this girl. As clear as day, I heard God say it won't work. Not because she was a bad person, but because she was the wrong person. I remember saying to God, "I can handle it. I am strong in your Word, and my willingness to set the example will be enough to change her heart." The truth was we were not equally yoked (2 Corinthians 6:14). I even found scriptures to justify doing what I wanted to do. I asked for God's approval, but the truth is I just wanted what I wanted. God said, "Don't come crying to me when it turns out bad." For ten years I set an example of excellence. I prayed and fasted for my family's spiritual health, I read my Bible, and I attended church, but in the long run, it wasn't enough. My efforts didn't change the fact that I was outside of God's will for my life. The deception was that I thought God should be obligated to fix my self-inflicted disaster. After all, I was leading a good example in the lives of my family.

God wanted good things for me. I just didn't want to wait on his timing. Satan's deception gave me a skewed perception of God's will for my situation, and I blamed God for my disobedience. The deception began to grow in my heart, leading me to the bondage of addiction. For three years I spent my days stoned while chasing every wrong relationship in search for what only God could give me. Satan doesn't care how he destroys us. He just wants to keep us from fulfilling our purpose in Christ. Any relationship that takes us away from God's best or keeps us from the fullness of God's promises should never be in our lives. God has an amazing plan and purpose for our lives (Jeremiah 29:11, Ephesians 3:20), way better than we can think or imagine. We have to seek God and wait for his timing. Otherwise, we are just deceived! Hope in the fulfillment of God's promises when we are walking in disobedience makes the heart sick (Proverbs 13:12- 14). Have a great day and know that Kim and I pray for God's best for each and every one of you daily.

Allow God

When we want to experience the fullness of God's promises in our lives, then we need to walk in the fullness of his Word (Ephesians 3:19). What?

These last few days have been rough for me. I literally worked seventy hours in three days, and the project I was doing was for the sole purpose of paying my rent. The guy I was doing work for was the perfect nightmare customer. He wanted everything for free, wasn't appreciative of my abilities and skills, was rude, and stiffed me on part of the bill. I was so angry because of his disregard to my excellence to go above and beyond giving him a quality job on such a small budget. As I was dealing with all these emotions, yesterday after church, my beautiful bride, whom I love with all my heart, said something that was in no way helping my stress level. On top of all, this I heard God remind me that just because the customer is acting like a jerk and isn't going to pay me, I still need to walk in love and forgive him (Matthew 5:44)! Say what? I blew up! I was a jerk toward this guy, and I said wrong things to my wife, so I blew it. I was so upset because God's Word says that everything I put my hands to would prosper, and this wasn't prospering by any means.

The real problem wasn't the promise or the truth that it presented; it was my anger that was based on fear, that God's Word wasn't doing what I wanted it to do (2 Timothy 1:7). My attitude and lack of trust was what was keeping my hands from prospering, not this guy being a jerk. The Word of God states that all things, good or bad, would work to my good because I love God and am called according to his purpose (Romans 8:28).

As the dust settled, I not only owed him an apology but I owed my loving wife an apology. I had to repent for having anger and a bad attitude. Satan was quick to whisper in my ear his disgust regarding my actions, bringing guilt and condemnation along for the ride (Revelation 12:10, Romans 8:1).

225

The moral of the story is this: we don't prosper because God's Word is true, but we prosper because our attitude in any situation is a reflection of God's promise. In order to experience the fullness of God's promise, I have to walk in the fullness of his Word. Love conquers all (1 Peter 4:8, Luke 6:27-38), and when it's all said and done, God is in control (Psalms 91). Kim and I love you and are believing God for good things for you! Have a super awesome day.

A New Car

The key to an abundant life is the Word of God (John 1:4, 10:10). What if your friend gave you the key to a brand-new car? Your friend gave you this luxury car, excited to see you enjoy the comforts and amenities it has to offer. You were super excited at first, but then you made the strangest statement: "I really don't think I have to put the keys in the ignition to enjoy this car." Every day you sat in the driveway enjoying the leather seats. Your friend walks up and says, "You know, those seats are heated, with memory and lumbar support." You reply, "It's all good. I don't need all that to enjoy these seats." Then your friend says, "If you put the key in the ignition, you can check out the radio. This radio is a surround sound with an MP3 player and a DVD player." Again, you respond with, "I can't believe I have to put the key in just to enjoy these different things. I should be able to enjoy everything about this car without the key. This is just not fair!" Your friend then asks how it drives. Again you comment by complaining, "This car is a piece of junk. It won't start. I just want to enjoy my car!" After six months of hearing you complain about your new car, you would begin to avoid the subject all together. Eventually your blessing would end up in a salvage yard, the final resting place of a blessing that never reached its full potential. If you went every day to the salvage yard mourning the loss of your gift knowing that you never experienced all that your car was designed to be, we would say you need some serious help.

As ridiculous as this all sounds we often live like this every day. The Word of God is the key to the abundant life Jesus came to give us (John 19:30). Jesus accomplished all this on the cross for my life and yours. The problem is that we want to experience all that was freely given to us but are offended that we would have to read and apply the Word of God in order to receive these very things (James 1:22).

The churches are full of defeated Christians. Many can tell others all about the blessing and what they can have. Most never attain the blessings in their own lives. We often never produce fruit that gives validity to the Word of God (Matthew 7:16). I can have a brand-new luxury car, but if I don't put the keys in the ignition, not only will I never go anywhere, but I won't be able to take anyone else anywhere.

The Word of God makes the impossible possible (Matthew 19:26). God makes a way where there is no way. God's Word gives us peace when the world has none to offer. God prospers everything we put our hands to do (Romans 15:13). The Word allows us to live in health when everyone else is fearful of the unknown (Proverbs 4:22). When we live our lives as a reflection of the Word of God, we prosper in every area of our lives physically, mentally, emotionally, and spiritually. People will notice and be led to freedom by the example we live (Proverbs 4:22, 2 Timothy 1:7).

Jesus said the truth will set us free (Psalms 33:4, John 8:32). The Word of God is truth. The more we apply God's Word to our lives, the more others will see truth. We will lead many to freedom as the truth breaks the chains of dark- ness that holds them prisoners in this lost and dying world (Psalms 107:14). We need to read our Bibles, applying all that God shows us (Romans 12:2). We should walk in the blessings God has for us and know that our lives are making a difference in the lives around us. Kim and I love you and are excited for God to finish what he has started in you. Have a great day.

A Life Outside the Box

As I continue reading in the book of Mark, it amazes me how the disciples put Jesus's abilities in a box, so to speak. Jesus's disciples had seen Jesus heal the sick, raise the dead, and so on (Matthew 8, Mark 5:21-43). When it came time to feed the five thousand, they weren't sure what to do (Matthew 14:13-21).

We in our own lives do the same thing. We believe in Jesus for salvation (John 3:16), but when it comes to the things in our lives that we think are too big, we don't know what to do. This is why it is so important that we read and learn the Word of God—so that we can accomplish all that God has called us to do in life (Hebrews 13:21, 2 Timothy 3:17).

First of all, the Bible states that in Christ, we can do all things because he is our strength (Philippians 4:13). The Word of God instructs us regarding every area of our lives (Proverbs 1:1-7) and how to overcome every problem we face. He is our provider, healer, and leader (Philippians 4:19, Psalms 147:3, 2 Corinthians 2:14). Jesus is our everything, our all in all, the beginning and the end (Revelation 22:13).

We should spend time learning who Jesus is and who we are in him (2 Timothy 2:15). We should allow our lives to be transformed into the beautiful reflection of all that Jesus is. Kim and I love you and are super excited to see you fulfill your purpose in all that God has for you. Have a great day!

A Need for a Savior

Good morning to all my friends and family. Much love and many blessings to you as we start our day. My words are few and basic today.

I was talking to God the other day and just thanking him for all that he has done in my life and the many people that I have been blessed with in my life to encourage and show his amazing love to— that would be all of you. I am grateful that God has trusted me with the privilege of encouraging you on a regular basis (Luke 16:10). My life is definitely richer having you a part of my life.

Today the message is this: God loves you and has amazing plans for your life (Jeremiah 29:11). If for whatever reason you have not asked Jesus into your heart, I encourage you to do so today (2 Corinthians 6:2). Life isn't about how good you are or how many things you do that are good but rather that we know and experience Jesus as our Savior.

Jesus is like having a Garmin. God is there to guide us and get us were we need to go safely (Psalms 119:105). There will be times we make wrong turns. It's no big deal because he just recalculates and gives us the directions needed to get back on the right road of life (Proverbs 24:16). Heaven is real, and there is only one way there (John 14:16). You recognize your need for a Savior/navigator. You ask him into your heart, allowing him to fill you with his peace of mind knowing he is in control (1 Corinthians 14:33).

I am super excited for the day the sky opens up and Jesus comes to take us home to heaven (1 Thessalonians 4:16). I have many friends who have crossed over, and I'm excited to see them and introduce all of you to all of them. Seek God in your life today and read your Bible so you can know and understand all that you are and what was made available to you (Romans 12:2). Kim and I love you and are excited to call you friends.

A New Beginning

Today is a new day. Live today on purpose! Don't just wait and see what the day brings (John 10:10). Let's use our time wisely and allow the love of God to permeate our lives. People should see our amazing can do attitudes. After all, we can do all things because Christ is our strength (Philippians 4:13). Jesus is in our hearts, and out of the abundance of the heart, the mouth speaks (Matthew 12:34). People should hear our encouraging words daily (Ephesians 4:29). If Jesus is the compassionate, encouraging force in our lives, then our lips should be an extension of that. Let your words be positive, uplifting, encouraging, and full of life (1 Corinthians 1:9).

Take time to start your day in fellowship with God. I am amazed that the creator of all things wants and desires our friendship. We should read our Bibles daily so we can be equipped to lead in truth (Romans 12:2, Ephesians 4:23). You can't lead in truth if you don't know truth. The Word of God is a powerful truth (John 17:17). Truth has the ability to set us free from the plans and schemes of all that Satan has for our lives (John 8:32, Ephesians 6:12). When we seek truth in our own lives, not only do we experience freedom, but it literally empowers us to give freedom (Matthew 10:5-8). In all that we do, we should learn to trust God, and our life will be complete! We will fulfill the purpose that God has for our lives. Always remember, if God can trust us to do the little things, he will use us to do the big things (Luke 16:10). Kim and I love you. Have super awesome day.

A Wagging Tongue

According to *Webster's* dictionary, a gossip is someone who often talks about the private details of other peoples lives. What does the Bible say about a gossip? Proverbs 20:19 states that we should have nothing to do with a person who gossiPsalms In 2 Timothy 3:3, it says that a gossip is someone without self-control, they are brutal, and they are haters of God.

When my boys were growing up, I always told them just because we know something doesn't mean we have to say it, even if it's true (Matthew 12:36-37). If we look at the story of Noah and the ark, the Bible states that when the flood was over, the first thing Noah did was plant a vineyard, make some wine, and get drunk (Genesis 9:20). Noah had three sons. One of his sons went into Noah's tent and saw his father naked and passed out on the floor. Rather than covering his father's shame, he went immediately to tell his brothers. The brothers took a blanket and backed into the tent and covered their father and scolded the other brother for shaming their father. That brother brought a curse on himself and his descendants because of his dishonor (Genesis 9:25).

The Bible states that our words should be encouraging, edifying, and uplifting and we should never gossip (Ephesians 4:29). The Bible states that the power of life and death are in the tongue (Proverbs 18:21). When we gossip, we are not displaying integrity to those around us. Gossip also destroys any opportunities we may have to minister in the future. Why? People know that if we will talk about others, then we can't be trusted when it comes to their issues. Gossip also keeps others from the goodness of God and can even cause them have offense not only toward us but toward God as well (Acts 24:16).

We as Christians should live our lives as a reflection of the Word of God (Proverbs 27:19) or who Jesus is. God takes our words very seriously. The Bible states that when we stand before God, we will have to give an account for all useless words that have come from our lips (Matthew 12:36-37).

The Bible states that God records our words. The whole purpose of Jesus's ministry was to restore relationship with man and God while bringing life to a dying world (2 Corinthians 5:18). We need to learn who we are according the Word of God so that we can have right fellowship with him (2 Timothy 2:15). This empowers us to go into the entire world and allow Jesus to shine through us (Matthew 28:16), bringing healing to the lost and dying.

We are surrounded daily with people who are hurting, who need peace, and who are searching for hope of a better life. The only way we can give them the love of God through us is if we have the love of God in us (James 1:18). So as you go through your day, stop and think, "Am I bringing healing with my words, or am I bringing hurt and destruction?" (Proverbs 18:21). The Bible states, "Today I set before you a blessing or a curse, life or death, choose life" (Deuteronomy 11-26, 30:19). Kim and I love you and are excited to watch you grow in God's love so that you can bring hope to a lost and dying world. Have a great day.

Abundance of Life

Jesus came to give us an abundance of life (John 10:10). Many times people relate this to money. However, the abundance of life is a life empowered to accomplish anything (Philippians 4:13). We as Christians, as we learn God's will for our lives through reading and applying his Word to our lives (1 John 5:14, James 4:3), we are literally empowered to accomplish anything, as the scripture states, "We can do all things through Christ because he is our strength" (Philippians 4:13). That in and of itself is worth more than any amount of money.

No matter what Satan brings against me, God will use it for his glory and my benefit (Romans 8:28). I don't have to worry about finances because God supplies all my needs according to his riches and glory in Christ Jesus (Philippians 4:6-7, Matthew 6:25-26). The list of God's greatness in our lives is endless. So what are you doing with your abundance of life (Titus 2:7)? The purpose of all that God is and supplies for us is to show others the possibilities when serving God.

When Satan throws opposition our way, it's nothing more than an opportunity to succeed (Romans 8:28), then using our opposition to be the strength for people in our lives that have no hope. If Satan can't keep you from experiencing victory in Christ, then his next best is keeping us from sharing our victory with others and setting the captives free (Mark 4:15, John 10:10). The Word of God states, "Freely you have received, so freely give" (Matthew 10:5-8). Are you living an abundant life? Are you allowing his abundance to change the lives around you? Live your live on purpose, and allow God to use you to set the captives free. Kim and I love you. Have a great day.

A Lie or Truth

How many times have we had someone tell us a lie regarding another person, and we just believe it rather than asking to make sure it wasn't true (1 Corinthians 13:6-7)? Why is it so easy to believe a lie, yet we question and dispute truth? Satan always lies about God's character and his faithfulness. Satan is the father of lies and knows no truth. When we are bombarded with problems, we need to remember that problems are false evidence that just appears real (John 8:44).

God's Word overcomes any and all problems Satan might through our way (Isaiah 55:11). Circumstances are nothing more than an elaborate lie of the enemy to persuade us to believe his lies (Philippians 4:13). The truth of the matter is, circumstances are just opportunities to succeed. God's Word states that all things, good or bad, work together for our good, because we love God and are called according to his purpose (Romans 8:28). Wow!

Here is the difference. When the devil says the sky is falling and we will probably die, he always shows us something that helps him to sell us his lies. On the other hand, truth says to believe what we can't see, and then God shows us his faithfulness (Hebrews 11:1). Satan shows us what he wants us to see because he operates out of manipulation! God asks for our trust and watches over his Word to perform it (Jeremiah 1:12).

God's promises are "yes" and "amen" (2 Corinthians 1:20). When opposition shows up and circumstances bombard our lives, look to the Word of God. Learn it, pray it, trust it, and know that if God is for us, then who can be against us (Romans 8:31)? The more we learn to trust in truth, the more freedom we can have in our lives, because we know that if it's all God, it's all good. The Bible tells us to use every opportunity to advance the gospel (Ephesians 5:15, 16).

If circumstances are really opportunities, then use them to apply God's Word, allowing our lives to be a reflection of God's faithfulness (Psalms 33:4). Wow, that just gets me so excited to know that through Christ, I can do anything and overcome anything (Philippians 4:13). Jesus paid a valuable price so that we can walk in victory. Kim and I love you and believe in you, and know that God has an amazing plan and purpose for your life. Have a super awesome day!

A Bright Future_____

Today can be the beginning of the rest of our lives (Ephesians 3:17-19). The rest of our lives can be the best of our lives! This is all made possible because of God's love. God gave all that he is so we can have all that he promises. God promises us that if we will acknowledge the sacrifice of his son's life and confess that he is our everything, then he will become our everything (John 3:16). And to sweeten the deal, he gave us his written Word to direct us in all his promises, encourage us, and teach us how to live a life free from stress, depression, hopelessness, and every destructive pattern that Satan puts in our path (Psalms 119:105).

God's Word is true, faithful, and just (Psalms 86:15). His promises are "yes" and "amen" (2 Corinthians 1:20). And he has an amazing plan and purpose for every one of our lives. God even tells us who our enemy is and informs us that Satan is the father of lies and knows no truth (John 8:44). We are literally equipped to conquer any and all obstacles in our lives (Philippians 4:13).

The only thing that can keep us from all that God has for us is us! The only power Satan has over us is the power of suggestion (Genesis 3:3, Matthew 4:1-5). Satan wants us to believe that God's Word isn't true. Never forget Satan is the father of lies and the truth is not in him (John 8:44). No matter what we have experienced, where our lives have taken us, the pain we have suffered, we can experience God and all that he has in store for us. Allow today to be the begging of the rest of your life. Because God's Word is true, the rest of our lives will be the best of our lives (Numbers 23:19). Kim and I love you and pray that every day you experience the fullness of God's plan and purpose for your lives. Have a great day!

A Continual Work of God

As Christians, problems are nothing more than opportunities for success (Romans 8:28). We know this because God promises us that all things, good or bad, work together for our good because we love God and are called according to his purpose.

I think a lot of times we as Christians have the mentality that we can get to a place where we no longer have trials in our lives. The bad news is the only way to live a life free of trials is to be dead and in heaven. The good news is that God's Word is amazing, and when we read and apply it, not only will God give us success in any situation but it also gives us the confidence to soar like an eagle (Psalms 119:105). The only way to enjoy the blessed life is to realize that every situation, good or bad, empowers us to set the standard in leading people in truth! Why? Because every situation is an opportunity to reflect God's faithfulness (Ephesians 5:8, 9).

A perfect example is my friend. He came out of a life of addiction and is now serving God while taking the time to learn and apply the Word of God in his life. As a result of his former lifestyle, he is going to have to sit in jail for a while. I realize that this isn't what he wants, but he realizes that if he has to be incarcerated, then there must be someone there that needs to know and under- stand the truth that my friend is now walking in.

When we rise above circumstance, we allow God to use us in any situation (Isaiah 40:31). Only then can we truly soar with the eagles. Rather than dreading our situation, we should ask ourselves how we can use this to bring glory and honor to God's holy name. This world is lost and dying and looking for truth every day. We need to rise above our situation and allow the Word of God to set the standard for victory in our lives and set the example of the power of God's faithfulness to those around us. We need to allow God to make a difference through our lives. Kim and I love you and are excited for what God is doing in you, through you, and for you! Have a great day!

A Blessing Blocker

I set before you a blessing or a curse (Deuteronomy 11:26). Choose the blessing, forgiveness, or unforgiveness! Unforgiveness is the biggest blessing blocker that Satan uses to keep us from experiencing all that God has for our lives. Forgiveness is the foundation of salvation, because without it, there is no salvation (Ephesians 1:7). The whole of salvation rests on the forgiveness or our sins and our right standing with Christ Jesus (2 Corinthians 5:21). God's grace, mercy, and forgiveness are the provisions that God has for our lives. The fullness of all that God wants and has for us is contingent on the forgiveness of our sins.

Satan knows this. This is why Satan wants his attack to become personal. Satan knows if he can get you operating outside of forgiveness, then he can have full access to our lives. I recently was faced with the decision of bitterness and unforgiveness because of someone who lied and tried to discredit my name and character. In reality, no one can discredit my character because my character is in Christ (Romans 8:33). It's not personal. When I made Jesus Lord of my life, I surrendered myself to him, and my life has become a reflection of who he is in all his goodness (Galatians 2:20). It's all about strategy. If I lose focus and allow the attack to become personal, then it gives root to unforgiveness and bitterness. I am no longer under the protection of God in my life, making me a sitting duck.

Unforgiveness opens us up to more deception and destruction in our lives (Matthew 18:23-35). When we realize our lives are in Christ, then no weapon formed against us will prosper (Isaiah 54:17). Every tongue that rises against us in judgment, God will prove to be in the wrong. Forgiveness gives us full access to the power of God in our lives, empowering us to overcome the plans and schemes of the enemy while living a victorious life in Christ Jesus (James 4:17). Satan wants to steal our joy, kill our purpose, and destroy our right standing with Jesus (John 10:10). Satan knows the power that is available to us through forgiveness. Satan wants to destroy any and all connection to the power of God in our lives. The Bible states for us to be as wise as a serpent (Matthew 10:17), know Satan's tactics (Revelation 12:11), and overcome him by the blood of the lamb and the Word that gives us our testimony. Kim and I love you and are excited for all that God has in store for your lives. Have a great day!

Hurry, Hurry, I'm Late, I'm Late

Have you ever gotten up and were running late, grabbed your phone, and off to work you went? You soon realize that your phone was almost dead and you didn't bring a charger? You need to use your phone for business. Your stress level leads you to start rearranging what calls you need to make, which ones are important, and which ones can wait. All in hopes of saving what little charge you have left for that one important call later in the day. Your efforts are all for nothing. The phone goes dead way before that important call comes through! We are just like that cell phone.

God has a specific plan and purpose for our lives today and many things that need accomplished. When we aren't plugged into God's Word, we don't have enough charge to accomplish his will for our lives, and people's lives aren't reached healed or loved! When we go day after day trying to use our phone on no charge, eventually the battery gets to the point where it won't hold a charge. This leaves us unable to fulfill our purpose when conducting business.

Don't be like that battery running every day on empty, never fulfilling your destiny in Christ! Get plugged in, read your Bible, and allow God to do awesome, mighty things in you, through you, and for you. Kim and I love you and pray for God's greatness in your lives. Have a great day.

The Ugliness of Serving Self

I recently met a lady that professes to go to church and have Jesus in her heart. Her life is anything but a reflection of Jesus's saving grace and his undying love. She hasn't said much in regard to her faith, but she has made comments regarding her pastor and his family. Don't be a name dropper! What is this? A name dropper is someone who doesn't live their life as a reflection of God's best but tells others that they are close to the main man JC himself.

Have you ever sat down to enjoy a hot piece of blackberry cobbler with a scoop of vanilla ice cream on top? By name, it sounds amazing! Just because it claims to be a blackberry cobbler doesn't mean it's good on the inside. You load up your spoon anticipating the sweet, hot berries and the cold treat of the rich vanilla ice cream. As the amazing combination hits your lips, your taste buds explode. You quickly realize this is not what you had in mind. The ice cream is sour, and the berries are rotten with the worst flavor you have ever tasted. Just because this cobbler got its fame from a name doesn't mean it's all we anticipate. How disappointing would this experience be?

There is nothing worse than meeting someone who is a Christian in name, but as you get to know them, they are selfish, self-centered, and controlling, with no evidence of God's love to be found in their lives. Not only is this disappointing, but it really leaves a bad taste in our mouths. The more people that we meet that are just a Christian in theory but not in reality, Satan begins to cause us to think that all Christians are hypocrites.

The purpose of reading and applying God's Word to our lives is so that the imperfections and the nasty, bitter things in our lives can be removed and replaced with the perfect reflection of all that God is. When we allow the Word of God to transform our lives, we are empowered to accomplish the impossible through his greatness, making us desirable to all. Everywhere Jesus went, people hung on his every word. Jesus brought hope to the hopeless and healing to the lost and dying. We should have that same response in our lives. People should know that we have the answers. People should be drawn to us in times of trouble and seek our prayers because we hear from God. Don't allow Satan to use you to embitter someone else's life. We should allow God's love to flow through us bringing hope and healing to all that know us. Have a great day. Kim and I love you.

Our Protection

The whole purpose of the lights and gates at a railroad crossing is to protect us from impending disaster! The RR isn't trying to be mean. They aren't trying to keep us from going forward in our journey. The RR is trying to assure safe passage and that you reach your destination safely! The other night there was a guy in Pacific, Missouri, who decided that he could ignore these safety gates, and in doing so, he was struck and killed by the train. The RR had taken every precaution to ensure this man's safety, and now he is dead.

God is like the RR in the sense that he has taken every precaution to ensure a safe journey in each and every one of our lives! The Bible is like the safety gates and flashing red lights at the crossing. It's not to hinder us; it's to guide and protect us from the plans and schemes of Satan and all his cohorts. Many times we think that we don't need the Word in our lives, only to experience the hardships of ignoring the precautions that are in place by God himself to ensure success in every area of our lives! It would be foolish of us to blame the RR if we get hit by a train if we ignore the safety features that were there for our protection. Always remember that our wrong decisions don't just affect us but they affect everyone involved. The conductor now has the gruesome memories of seeing a man's life snuffed out, the bystanders also are directly affected with the thoughts of such a horrific scene, and the family members of the deceased man are all mourning for his loss of life and all for nothing.

This whole situation could have been avoided. God instructs us how to be successful in every area of our lives and how to overcome adversity by reading and applying his Word to our lives. So take the time to seek God today, read your Bible, and live your life in a way that your life is a positive experience for all those who are in your life circle rather than infecting their lives with avoidable disasters in your own life. God wants the very best for your life. Kim and I are cheering for you. Have a great day!

Practical

According to *Webster's* dictionary, the meaning of *practical* is "likely to succeed, reasonable to do or use. Appropriate or suited for actual use." Jesus was followed everywhere he went. Hundreds of thousands of people gathered to hear the words that Jesus spoke. Jesus gave truth in such a way that people were hungry for every word he spoke. Jesus wasn't educated to the world's standards. He was just the son of a carpenter that had an amazing relationship with his Heavenly Father. Often when Jesus couldn't be found, it's because he had retreated to a quiet place in order to spend time with his Father. This was done so that we could have an example in how to seek Jesus and his strength in our own lives. Jesus always spoke in such a way that people could understand. Jesus spoke in simple stories. Jesus always spoke so the working man could understand.

Most of the people who were listening to his messages were uneducated farmers and fisherman. Jesus utilized what the people knew and never judged anyone. Jesus always saw people for their potential and never for their problems. Jesus encouraged many to fulfill their destiny. The only people who truly had a problem with what Jesus was saying were the religious people, those that thought they knew what it meant to serve God. Jesus referred to these people as a brood of serpents. God has placed people in our lives, and we might be the only Jesus they will ever see. Their destiny may literally be in our hands.

I am always amazed that God has entrusted us with the most precious thing in this world: the souls of the people that are in our lives! Our job isn't to change people. Our job is to love them. When they see God's love through us, we become the perfect reflection of God's peace, love, mercy, compassion, joy, patience, kindness, goodness, and self-control. God's job is to take the consistency of our lives through his love and help people to understand the fullness of his saving grace. Never forget we are not responsible for what people do with our goodness. We just need to be responsible and love people! Have a great day, and always remember we can do all things through Christ, who is our strength. Kim and I love you.

The Word of God Is Not a Spare Tire

Sometimes we go through life, and we carry God in our spare compartment just in case we find ourselves in that situation that requires immediate attention. Perhaps in divorce, the boss that's a jerk, the financial situation that came out of nowhere, a troubled child, or a sudden loss. We often look to God to fix our untimely situation or emergency.

We should look at God's Word as our source. When we read and apply God's Word, we are literally doing preventive maintenance. God's Word is the steering wheel of our lives. When God is steering, then when my unexpected trouble comes, I'm safe in his direction. His Word is and should be our everything. God's Word gives us all that we need to overcome Satan's plans and schemes for our lives. The Word of God is our all in all.

God instructs us to read our Bible daily. Is it possible he knows something we don't? Seek direction through his Word daily. Strive to walk in all that is avail- able to us through what Jesus accomplished on the cross. God loves us and has an amazing plan and purpose for our lives. When we ask Jesus into our lives, we fulfill our destiny. When we apply his Word and walk in all that he has for us, we fulfill our purpose. Kim and I love you. Have a great day.

247

Living in the Fullness of Life

Jesus made an amazing statement, "I did not come to condemn the world but to give life and life more abundantly" (John 3:17). Jesus never looks at our imperfections before or after salvation. Jesus only sees our potential in what he has accomplished on the cross. How do we know this? Jesus is love, and true love finds no fault (1 Corinthians 13). The Bible states that love is the fruit that is produced by the spirit of God. Love is patient. Love is kind. It doesn't envy or boast, nor is it proud. Love does not dishonor, it is not self-seeking, and it is not easily angered. Love doesn't delight in evil but always rejoices in truth. Love always protects, always trust, and never fails. Love conquers all! It's because of God's love that Jesus willingly gave his life for us. He didn't have to. The Bible states that Jesus could have called down twelve legions of angels to get him off the cross, but he chose to be led by love (Matthew 26:53. The Bible says that there is no greater love than when we lay our lives down for others (John 15:13).

How can we do this? By allowing our lives to be a reflection of love. This allows the fruit of the spirit to permeate our lives! We are all subject to imperfections, but love is a choice. The truth of the matter is, there are people in each of our lives that need and depend on our willingness to put our own thoughts and ways of doing things down while embracing love.

My friend of twenty-six years died the other day, and as I lay in bed thinking about my example of Christ in his life, I realized I have not been consistent. Ultimately he was responsible for the decisions he made in his own life, but I could have been so much more of a friend. After all, we are talking about eternity! I can't lose time anguishing over what I should have been. I do realize that my life does make a difference. It is so important that I stay consistent in allowing God's love to shine through me! The hardest part of calling me his friend is not knowing where he is spending eternity or knowing that I was constant in my example of what true love is. I hope that he experienced the opportunity to know Christ before he died.

What kind of difference is your life making? Are you leading those around you to know and understand the saving grace of Jesus Christ? We can be powerful or pitiful. Choose to let your life be a powerful force in the lives around you. Kim and I love you and are grateful to know that you are making a difference in this world! Have a great day.

Right Choices

Determination and consistency to make right choices bring good things in to our lives. Have you ever wanted the results of the gym on January 1? You are determined to apply yourself, and a week later your determination fizzles out. You realize that those six-pack abs are hard work.

The key to success when seeking God in our lives is getting into a good routine or simply being consistent. I can't walk in truth if I don't know truth. Truth only comes from reading our Bibles. We can't stand on God's promises if we don't know what they are. We can't encourage others if we don't know how to get encouragement ourselves.

God has amazing plans for our lives (Jeremiah 29:11). God wants to help us succeed in every aspect of our lives. God wants to bless us beyond our wildest imagination (Ephesians 3:20). When the rubber meets the road, it's up to us whether we fail or we succeed. Don't settle for less when the sky is the limit. Seek God today, talk to him, read his Word, and expect good things in your life today. Kim and I love you and are super excited to see God working in your life while accomplishing greatness and changing the lives around you. Have a great day!

A Shot of God's Word

Today is a new day, and God's mercies are new every morning (Lamentations 3:22-23). God makes a way where there seems to be no way (Philippians 2:13). God gives us favor with people. Everything we put our hands to do will prosper (Deuteronomy 28:8). God gives his angels charge over us to guide and protect us. We can do all things because Jesus is our strength (Philippians 4:13).

God's greatest desire is our friendship (1 Corinthians 1:9)! That's what we were created for, to experience God's goodness and his mercy firsthand. Why? So that we can have an abundance of life and take that life and share it with others, giving them the same hope and healing that Jesus so freely provided for us (Matthew 10:8). Wow! The message isn't hard, nor is it complicated (Matthew 11:3). In fact, Jesus said we should have a childlike mentality when considering the good news of salvation and all that he has made available to us (Luke 18:17). Have a super awesome day, walk in love, and change lives while giving hope. Thank God for his amazing friendship. Kim and love you and pray for you every day.

Good Morning!

Today is a new day for everyone. If you are a believer and working on fulfilling your purpose in this earth, then today is a new beginning to reach the lost and dying, love the brokenhearted, using every opportunity to advance the gospel of his holy name. If you know Christ but have stepped back or lost your way due to you falling in your faith or you feeling guilty about something you did or didn't do, the Bible states that God's mercies are new every morning. God loves you and only sees your potential in Christ. So drop the guilt and shame for there is no condemnation in Christ. The Bible states that a righteous man may fall seven times, but he gets back up. Don't allow Satan to hold you in a place of shame when in reality, anything coming out of his mouth is a lie, and he knows no truth.

If today you are reading this and you have never asked Jesus into your heart, then this new beginning is just for you. The Bible states that today is the day of salvation. God has an amazing plan and purpose for your life. God loves you and wants only the best for you. The creator of all things thinks you are special and longs to have relationship with you. Just say,

> "Father, thank you for your love, mercy, grace, and compassion. Thank you for giving your son to die for my sins. Jesus, come into my heart and make me brand- new. I don't exactly understand how all this works, but please reveal yourself to me and help me learn and become all that you desire for me. Thank you for all that you are. In Jesus's name, amen."

Congratulations, you are born again. Today is the beginning of the rest of your life, and from this day forward, you have a purpose. Begin to seek God out in your life, and read your Bible daily. Start in the book of John; that's after Luke. Pray and ask God to open your eyes and reveal the Bible to you. If you don't understand the translation, you have to get something you do understand. The New Living Translation is a good one to begin with. Kim and I love you and are super excited for you to fulfill your destiny in Christ and your purpose in this earth. Have a great day.

Kirk Ratliff

*** Subject Index***

Pain & Suffering

Power & Opposition

The Simplicity of a Practical Jesus

Salvation

Satan & Sin

Truth

Trust & Peace

*** Scripture Reference Index***

The Simplicity of a Practical Jesus

The Simplicity of a Practical Jesus

*** About the Author ***

Kirk was born in St. Louis, Missouri, and has always had a flare for the creative process. He always excelled in art and is able to use any medium when expressing his creativeness. He spent sixteen years as a body man and ten years building custom cars and resto mods. He started in the auto body industry and quickly excelled in every step of the process. In 2004, Kirk opened Jc's Kustom Creations and started building cars with his oldest son, Jesse. In 2015, Kirk began writing a daily blog, which led to his first book, *The Simplicity of a Practical Jesus*. Kirk is currently working on his second book, *When Dreams Come True*. Kirk married his soul mate, Kimberly Sue Ratliff, in 2013.

Made in the USA
Columbia, SC
23 April 2021